RIGHTS OF MAN

Additional volumes in Prometheus's
Great Books in Philosophy Series

The Republic
by Plato

Politics
by Aristotle

The Nicomachean Ethics
by Aristotle

The Prince
by Niccolo Machiavelli

*Fundamental Principles of the
Metaphysic of Morals*
by Immanuel Kant

Second Treatise on Civil Government
by John Locke

On Liberty
by John Stuart Mill

The Subjection of Women
by John Stuart Mill

Utilitarianism
by John Stuart Mill

RIGHTS
OF MAN

BEING AN ANSWER TO MR. BURKE'S ATTACK ON THE FRENCH REVOLUTION

THOMAS PAINE

PROMETHEUS BOOKS

700 East Amherst St., Buffalo, New York 14215

Published 1987 Prometheus Books
700 East Amherst Street, Buffalo, New York 14215

Library of Congress Catalog Number: 86-64007
ISBN 0-87975-379-X

THOMAS PAINE was born in Thetford, County of Norfolk, England, on January 29, 1737. His Quaker upbringing nurtured in him a deep concern for the human struggle to be free from oppression, a struggle that would culminate in each person being able to determine his own individual destiny. Paine's subsequent political involvement in England became the substantive grounding for the radical party.

In 1774, at the age of thirty seven, Paine left England for a new life in America. There he was enthusiastically embraced as the author of *Common Sense*, a popular essay written in support of independence for the Colonies. Thirteen years later he would return to his native England to take up the cause of the French Revolution with the publication of his famous *Rights of Man*. Though he received acclaim in France, his views were roundly condemned in England. Paine later moved to France, where his political involvements eventually saw him fall victim to the Reign of Terror. His imprisonment was productively spent completing a third major work, *The Age of Reason*.

The final years of Paine's life were spent in relative obscurity in America, the country for whose independence he was such a gallant spokesman. He died in New York on June 8, 1809.

Contents

PART I

[DEDICATION]

To George Washington

PRESIDENT OF THE UNITED STATES OF AMERICA

SIR,

I PRESENT you a small treatise in defense of those principles of freedom which your exemplary virtue hath so eminently contributed to establish. That the rights of man may become as universal as your benevolence can wish, and that you may enjoy the happiness of seeing the New World regenerate the Old, is the prayer of

Sir

Your much obliged, and

Obedient humble servant,

THOMAS PAINE

PREFACES

1. Preface to the French Edition

The astonishment which the French Revolution has caused throughout Europe should be considered from two different points of view: first as it affects foreign people, secondly as it affects their governments.

The cause of the French people is that of all Europe, or rather of the whole world; but the governments of all those countries are by no means favorable to it. It is important that we should never lose sight of this distinction. We must not confuse the peoples with their governments; especially not the English people with its government.

The government of England is no friend to the revolution of France. Of this we have sufficient proofs in the thanks given by that weak and witless person, the Elector of Hanover, sometimes called the King of England, to Mr. Burke for the insults heaped on it in his book, and in the malevolent comments of the English Minister, Mr. Pitt, in his speeches in Parliament.

In spite of the professions of sincerest friendship found in the official correspondence of the English government with that of France, its conduct gives the lie to all its declarations and shows us clearly that it is not a court to be trusted, but an insane court, plunging in all the quarrels and intrigues of Europe in quest of a war to satisfy its folly and countenance its extravagance.

The English nation, on the contrary, is very favorably disposed towards the French Revolution and to the progress of liberty in the whole world; and this feeling will become more general in England as the intrigues and artifices of its government are better known, and the principles of the revolution better understood. The French should know that most English newspapers are directly in the pay of government or, if indirectly connected with it, always under its orders; and that these papers constantly distort and attack the revolution in France in order to deceive the nation. But, as it is impossible long to prevent the prevalence of truth, the daily falsehoods of those papers no longer have the desired effect.

To be convinced that the voice of truth has been stifled in England, the world needs only to be told that the government regards and prosecutes as a libel that which it should protect.[1] This outrage on morality is called *law*, and judges are found wicked enough to inflict penalties on truth.

[1]The main and uniform maxim of the judges is, the greater the truth the greater the libel.

The English government presents just now a curious phenomenon. Seeing that the French and English nations are getting rid of the prejudices and false notions formerly entertained against each other, and which have cost them so much money, that government seems to be placarding its need of a foe; for unless it finds one somewhere, no pretext exists for the enormous revenue and taxation now deemed necessary.

Therefore it seeks in Russia the enemy it has lost in France, and appears to say to the universe, or to say to itself: "If nobody will be so kind as to become my foe, I shall need no more fleets or armies, and shall be forced to reduce my taxes. The American war enabled me to double the taxes; the Dutch business to add more; the Nootka humbug gave me a pretext for raising three millions sterling more; but unless I can make an enemy of Russia the harvest from wars will end. I was the first to incite Turk against Russian, and now I hope to reap a fresh crop of taxes."

If the miseries of war and the flood of evils it spreads over a country did not check all inclination to mirth and turn laughter into grief, the frantic conduct of the government of England would only excite ridicule. But it is impossible to banish from one's mind the images of suffering which the contemplation of such vicious policy presents. To reason with governments, as they have existed for ages, is to argue with brutes. It is only from the nations themselves that reforms can be expected. There ought not now to exist any doubt that the peoples of France, England, and America, enlightened and enlightening each other, shall henceforth be able, not merely to give the world an example of good government, but by their united influence enforce its practice.

2. *Preface to the English Edition*

From the part Mr. Burke took in the American Revolution it was natural that I should consider him a friend to mankind; and as our acquaintance commenced on that ground, it would have been more agreeable to me to have had cause to continue in that opinion than to change it.

At the time Mr. Burke made his violent speech last winter in the English Parliament against the French Revolution and the National Assembly, I was in Paris, and had written to him but a short time before to inform him how prosperously matters were going on. Soon after this I saw his advertisement of the pamphlet he intended to publish: As the attack was to be made in a language but little studied and less understood in France, and as everything suffers by translation, I promised some of the friends of the Revolution in that country that whenever Mr. Burke's pamphlet came forth, I would answer it. This appeared to me the more necessary to be done when I saw the flagrant misrepresentations which Mr. Burke's pamphlet contains; and that while it is an outrageous abuse on the French Revolution and the principles of Liberty, it is an imposition on the rest of the world.

I am the more astonished and disappointed at this conduct in Mr. Burke, as (from the circumstances I am going to mention) I had formed other expectations.

I had seen enough of the miseries of war to wish it might never more have existence in the world, and that some other mode might be found out to settle the differences that should occasionally arise in the neighborhood of nations. This certainly might be done if courts were disposed to set honestly about it, or if countries were enlightened enough not to be made the dupes of courts. The people of America had been bred up in the same prejudices against France which at that time characterized the people of England; but experience and an acquaintance with the French nation have most effectually shown to the Americans the falsehood of those prejudices; and I do not believe that a more cordial and confidential intercourse exists between any two countries than between America and France.

When I came to France in the spring of 1787, the Archbishop of Toulouse was then Minister, and at that time highly esteemed. I became much acquainted with the private secretary of that minister, a man of an enlarged benevolent heart; and found that his sentiments and my own perfectly agreed with respect to the madness of war and the wretched impolicy of two nations, like

England and France, continually worrying each other to no
other end than that of a mutual increase of burdens and taxes.
That I might be assured I had not misunderstood him, nor he
me, I put the substance of our opinions into writing and sent it
to him; subjoining a request, that if I should see among the
people of England any disposition to cultivate a better understanding between the two nations than had hitherto prevailed,
how far I might be authorized to say that the same disposition
prevailed on the part of France? He answered me by letter in
the most unreserved manner, and that not for himself only, but
for the minister with whose knowledge the letter was declared
to be written.

I put this letter into the hands of Mr. Burke almost three
years ago, and left it with him, where it still remains; hoping,
and at the same time naturally expecting, from the opinion I
had conceived of him, that he would find some opportunity
of making good use of it for the purpose of removing those
errors and prejudices which two neighboring nations, from
the want of knowing each other, had entertained to the injury
of both.

When the French Revolution broke out it certainly afforded
to Mr. Burke an opportunity of doing some good had he been
disposed to it; instead of which, no sooner did he see the old
prejudices wearing away, than he immediately began sowing
the seeds of a new inveteracy, as if he were afraid that England
and France would cease to be enemies. That there are men in
all countries who get their living by war, and by keeping up
the quarrels of nations, is as shocking as it is true; but when
those who are concerned in the government of a country make
it their study to sow discord and cultivate prejudices between
nations, it becomes more unpardonable.

With respect to a paragraph in this work alluding to Mr.
Burke's having a pension, the report has been some time in circulation, at least two months; and as a person is often the last
to hear what concerns him the most to know, I have mentioned
it, that Mr. Burke may have an opportunity of contradicting
the rumor, if he thinks proper.

[ON BURKE'S "REFLECTIONS ON THE FRENCH REVOLUTION"]

Among the incivilities by which nations or individuals provoke and irritate each other, Mr. Burke's pamphlet on the French revolution is an extraordinary instance. Neither the people of France nor the national assembly were troubling themselves about the affairs of England or the English parliament; and why Mr. Burke should commence an unprovoked attack upon them, both in parliament and in public, is a conduct that cannot be pardoned on the score of manners, nor justified on that of policy.

There is scarcely an epithet of abuse to be found in the English language with which Mr. Burke has not loaded the French nation and the national assembly. Everything which rancor, prejudice, ignorance, or knowledge could suggest, are poured forth in the copious fury of near four hundred pages. In the strain and on the plan Mr. Burke was writing, he might have wrote on to as many thousand. When the tongue or the pen is let loose in a frenzy of passion, it is the man and not the subject that becomes exhausted.

Hitherto Mr. Burke has been mistaken and disappointed in the opinions he had formed on the affairs of France; but such is the ingenuity of his hope, or the malignancy of his despair, that it furnishes him with new pretenses to go on. There was a time when it was impossible to make Mr. Burke believe there would be any revolution in France. His opinion then was that the French had neither spirit to undertake it nor fortitude to support it; and now that there is one, he seeks an escape by condemning it.

Not sufficiently content with abusing the national assembly, a great part of his work is taken up with abusing Dr. Price (one of the best-hearted men that exists) and the two societies in England, known by the name of the Revolution and the Constitutional societies.

Dr. Price had preached a sermon on the 4th of November, 1789, being the anniversary of what is called in England the revolution, which took place in 1688. Mr. Burke, speaking of this sermon, says, "the political divine proceeds dogmatically to assert that, by the principles of the revolution, the people of England have acquired three fundamental rights:

1st, To choose our own governors.

2d, To cashier them for misconduct.

3d, To frame a government for ourselves."

Dr. Price does not say that the right to do these things exists in this or in that person, or in this or in that description of persons, but that it exists in the *whole*—that it is a right resident in the nation. Mr. Burke, on the contrary, denies that such a right exists in the nation, either in whole or in part, or that it exists anywhere; and what is still more strange and marvellous, he says that "the people of England utterly disclaim such right, and that they will resist the practical assertion of it with their lives and fortunes." That men will take up arms, and spend their lives and fortunes *not* to maintain their rights, but to maintain that they have *not* rights, is an entire new species of discovery, and suited to the paradoxical genius of Mr. Burke.

The method which Mr. Burke takes to prove that the people of England have no such rights, and that such rights do not exist in the nation, either in whole or in part, or anywhere at all, is of the same marvellous and monstrous kind with what he has already said; for his arguments are that the persons, or the generation of persons, in whom they did exist are dead, and with them the right is dead also. To prove this, he quotes a declaration made by parliament about a hundred years ago to William and Mary in these words: "The lords spiritual and temporal, and commons, do, in the name of the people aforesaid (meaning the people of England then living) most humbly and faithfully *submit* themselves, their *heirs* and *posterity*, FOREVER." He also quotes a clause of another act of parliament made in the same reign, the terms of which, he says, "bind us (meaning the people of that day), our *heirs* and our *posterity*, to *them*, their *heirs* and *posterity*, to the end of time."

Mr. Burke considers his point sufficiently established by producing those clauses, which he enforces by saying that they ex-

clude the right of the nation *forever:* and not yet content with
making such declarations, repeated over and over again, he
further says "that if the people of England possessed such a
right before the revolution" (which he acknowledges to have
been the case, not only in England, but throughout Europe, at
an early period), "yet that the *English nation* did, at the time of
the revolution, most solemnly renounce and abdicate it, for
themselves, and *for all their posterity forever.*"

As Mr. Burke occasionally applies the poison drawn from his
horrid principles (if it is not a profanation to call them by the
name of principles) not only to the English nation, but to the
French revolution and the national assembly, and charges that
august, illuminated and illuminating body of men with the
epithet of *usurpers,* I shall, *sans cérémonie,* place another system
of principles in opposition to his.

The English parliament of 1688 did a certain thing which for
themselves and their constituents they had a right to do, and
which appeared right should be done; but in addition to this
right, which they possessed by delegation, *they set up another
right by assumption,* that of binding and controlling posterity to
the end of time. The case, therefore, divides itself into two
parts; the right which they possessed by delegation, and the
right which they set up by assumption. The first is admitted;
but with respect to the second, I reply:

There never did, nor never can exist a parliament, or any
description of men, or any generation of men, in any country,
possessed of the right or the power of binding or controlling
posterity to the "end of time," or of commanding forever how
the world shall be governed, or who shall govern it; and therefore all such clauses, acts, or declarations, by which the makers
of them attempt to do what they have neither the right nor the
power to do, nor the power to execute, are in themselves null
and void. Every age and generation must be as free to act for
itself, *in all cases,* as the ages and generations which preceded it.
The vanity and presumption of governing beyond the grave is
the most ridiculous and insolent of all tyrannies. Man has no
property in man; neither has any generation a property in the

generations which are to follow. The parliament or the people of 1688, or of any other period, had no more right to dispose of the people of the present day, or to bind or to control them *in any shape whatever*, than the parliament or the people of the present day have to dispose of, bind, or control those who are to live a hundred or a thousand years hence. Every generation is and must be competent to all the purposes which its occasions require. It is the living and not the dead that are to be accommodated. When man ceases to be, his power and his wants cease with him; and having no longer any participation in the concerns of this world, he has no longer any authority in directing who shall be its governors, or how its government shall be organized, or how administered.

I am not contending for, nor against, any form of government, nor for nor against any party, here or elsewhere. That which a whole nation chooses to do, it has a right to do. Mr. Burke denies it. Where then does the right exist? I am contending for the right of the *living*, and against their being willed away, and controlled and contracted for, by the manuscript-assumed authority of the dead; and Mr. Burke is contending for the authority of the dead over the rights and freedom of the living. There was a time when kings disposed of their crowns by will upon their deathbeds, and consigned the people, like beasts of the field, to whatever successor they appointed. This is now so exploded as scarcely to be remembered, and so monstrous as hardly to be believed; but the parliamentary clauses upon which Mr. Burke builds his political church are of the same nature.

The laws of every country must be analogous to some common principle. In England, no parent or master, nor all the authority of parliament, omnipotent as it has called itself, can bind or control the personal freedom even of an individual beyond the age of twenty-one years: on what ground of right then could the parliament of 1688, or any other parliament, bind all posterity forever?

Those who have quitted the world, and those who are not arrived yet in it, are as remote from each other as the utmost stretch of mortal imagination can conceive: what possible obligation then can exist between them, what rule or principle can be laid down, that two nonentities, the one out of existence, and the other not in, and who never can meet in this world, that the one should control the other to the end of time?

In England it is said that money cannot be taken out of the pockets of the people without their consent: but who authorized, and who could authorize, the parliament of 1688 to control and take away the freedom of posterity, and limit and confine their rights of acting in certain cases forever, who were not in existence to give or withhold their consent?

A greater absurdity cannot present itself to the understanding of man than what Mr. Burke offers to his readers. He tells them, and he tells the world to come, that a certain body of men, who existed a hundred years ago, made a law, and that there does not now exist in the nation, nor never will, nor never can, a power to alter it. Under how many subtleties, or absurdities, has the divine right to govern been imposed on the credulity of mankind! Mr. Burke has discovered a new one, and he has shortened his journey to Rome by appealing to the power of this infallible parliament of former days; and he produces what it has done as of divine authority; for that power must be certainly more than human, which no human power to the end of time can alter.

But Mr. Burke has done some service, not to his cause, but to his country, by bringing those clauses into public view. They serve to demonstrate how necessary it is at all times to watch against the attempted encroachment of power, and to prevent its running to excess. It is somewhat extraordinary that the offense for which James II was expelled, that of setting up power by *assumption*, should be re-acted under another shape and form by the parliament that expelled him. It shows that the rights of man were but imperfectly understood at the revolution; for certain it is that the right which that parliament set up by *assumption* (for by delegation it had not, and could not have it, because none could give it) over the persons and freedom of posterity forever, was of the same tyrannical, unfounded kind which

James attempted to set up over the parliament and the nation, and for which he was expelled. The only difference is (for in principle they differ not) that the one was a usurper over the living, and the other over the unborn; and as the one has no better authority to stand upon than the other, both of them must be equally null and void, and of no effect.

From what or whence does Mr. Burke prove the right of any human power to bind posterity forever? He has produced his clauses; but he must produce also his proofs that such a right existed, and show how it existed. If it ever existed, it must now exist; for whatever appertains to the nature of man cannot be annihilated by man. It is the nature of man to die, and he will continue to die as long as he continues to be born. But Mr. Burke has set up a sort of political Adam in whom all posterity are bound forever; he must therefore prove that his Adam possessed such a power or such a right.

The weaker any cord is, the less it will bear to be stretched, and the worse is the policy to stretch it, unless it is intended to break it. Had a person contemplated the overthrow of Mr. Burke's positions, he would have proceeded as Mr. Burke has done. He would have magnified the authorities, on purpose to have called the *right* of them into question; and the instant the question of right was started, the authorities must have been given up.

It requires but a very small glance of thought to perceive that although laws made in one generation often continue in force through succeeding generations, yet they continue to derive their force from the consent of the living. A law not repealed continues in force, not because it *cannot* be repealed, but because it *is not* repealed; and the non-repealing passes for consent.

But Mr. Burke's clauses have not even this qualification in their favor. They become null by attempting to become immortal. The nature of them precludes consent. They destroy the right which they *might* have by grounding it on a right which they *cannot* have. Immortal power is not a human right, and therefore cannot be a right of parliament. The parliament of 1688 might as well have passed an act to have authorized itself to live forever, as to make their authority live forever. All, therefore, that can be said of them is that they are a formality of words, of as much import as if those who used them had addressed a congratulation to themselves and, in the oriental style of antiquity, had said, O! parliament, live forever!

The circumstances of the world are continually changing, and the opinions of men change also; and as government is for the living and not for the dead, it is the living only that has any right in it. That which may be thought right and found convenient in one age may be thought wrong and found inconvenient in another. In such cases, who is to decide, the living or the dead?

As almost one hundred pages of Mr. Burke's book are employed upon these clauses, it will consequently follow that if the clauses themselves, so far as they set up an *assumed, usurped* dominion over posterity forever, are unauthoritative, and in their nature null and void, that all his voluminous inferences and declamation drawn therefrom, or founded thereon, are null and void also: and on this ground I rest the matter.

We now come more particularly to the affairs of France. Mr. Burke's book has the appearance of being written as instruction to the French nation; but if I may permit myself the use of an extravagant metaphor, suited to the extravagance of the case, it is darkness attempting to illuminate light.

While I am writing this, there is accidentally before me some proposals for a declaration of rights by the Marquis de la Fayette (I ask his pardon for using his former address, and do it only for distinction's sake) to the national assembly on the 11th of July, 1789, three days before the taking of the Bastile; and I cannot but be struck how opposite the sources are from which that gentleman and Mr. Burke draw their principles. Instead of referring to musty records and mouldy parchments to prove that the rights of the living are lost, "renounced and abdicated forever" by those who are now no more, as Mr. Burke has done, M. de la Fayette applies to the living world, and emphatically says, "Call to mind the sentiments which nature has en-

graved in the heart of every citizen, and which take a new force
when they are solemnly recognized by all:—for a nation to love
liberty, it is sufficient that she knows it; and to be free, it is sufficient that she wills it." How dry, barren, and obscure, is the
source from which Mr. Burke labors; and how ineffectual,
though embellished with flowers, is all his declamation and his
argument, compared with these clear, concise, and soul-ani-
mating sentiments: few and short as they are, they lead on to a
vast field of generous and manly thinking, and do not finish,
like Mr. Burke's periods, with music in the ear and nothing in
the heart.

As I have introduced the mention of M. de la Fayette, I will
take the liberty of adding an anecdote respecting his farewell
address to the congress of America in 1783, and which occurred
fresh to my mind when I saw Mr. Burke's thundering attack on
the French revolution. M. de la Fayette went to America at
an early period of the war and continued a volunteer in her
service to the end. His conduct through the whole of that enterprise is one of the most extraordinary that is to be found in the
history of a young man, scarcely then twenty years of age.
Situated in a country that was like the lap of sensual pleasure,
and with the means of enjoying it, how few are there to be found
who would exchange such a scene for the woods and wilderness
of America, and pass the flowery years of youth in unprofitable
danger and hardship! But such is the fact. When the war
ended and he was on the point of taking his final departure, he
presented himself to congress, and contemplating, in his affectionate farewell, the revolution he had seen, expressed himself
in these words: "*May this great monument raised to Liberty serve
as a lesson to the oppressor and an example to the oppressed!*"
When this address came to the hands of Dr. Franklin who was
then in France, he applied to Count Vergennes to have it in-
serted in the French gazette, but never could obtain his consent.
The fact was that Count Vergennes was an aristocratical despot
at home, and dreaded the example of the American revolution in
France as certain other persons now dread the example of the
French revolution in England; and Mr. Burke's tribute of fear

(for in this light his book must be considered) runs parallel with Count Vergennes' refusal. But to return more particularly to his work.

"We have seen (says Mr. Burke) the French rebel against a mild and lawful monarch with more fury, outrage, and insult than any people has been known to raise against the most illegal usurper, or the most sanguinary tyrant." This is one among a thousand other instances in which Mr. Burke shows that he is ignorant of the springs and principles of the French revolution.

It was not against Louis XVI but against the despotic principle of the government that the nation revolted. These principles had not their origin in him, but in the original establishment, many centuries back; and they were become too deeply rooted to be removed, and the Augean stable of parasites and plunderers too abominably filthy to be cleansed, by anything short of a complete and universal revolution.

When it becomes necessary to do a thing, the whole heart should join in the measure, or it should not be attempted. That crisis was then arrived, and there remained no choice but to act with determined vigor or not to act at all. The king was known to be the friend of the nation, and this circumstance was favorable to the enterprise. Perhaps no man bred up in the style of an absolute king ever possessed a heart so little disposed to the exercise of that species of power as the present king of France. But the principles of the government itself still remained the same. The monarch and monarchy were distinct and separate things; and it was against the established despotism of the latter, and not against the person or principles of the former, that the revolt commenced, and the revolution has been carried on.

Mr. Burke does not attend to this distinction between men and principles, and therefore he does not see that a revolt may take place against the despotism of the latter, while there lies no charge of despotism against the former.

The natural moderation of Louis XVI contributed nothing to alter the hereditary despotism of the monarchy. All the tyrannies of former reigns, acted under that hereditary despotism, were still liable to be revived in the hands of a successor. It

of his rights. As to the manner in which the world has been governed from that day to this, it is no further any concern of ours than to make a proper use of the errors or the improvements which the history of it presents. Those who lived a hundred or a thousand years ago were then moderns as we are now. They had *their* ancients and those ancients had others, and we also shall be ancients in our turn. If the mere name of antiquity is to govern in the affairs of life, the people who are to live a hundred or a thousand years hence may as well take us for a precedent, as we make a precedent of those who lived a hundred or a thousand years ago. The fact is that portions of antiquity, by proving everything, establish nothing. It is authority against authority all the way till we come to the divine origin of the rights of man at the creation. Here our inquiries find a resting-place, and our reason finds a home. If a dispute about the rights of man had arisen at the distance of a hundred years from the creation, it is to this source of authority they must have referred, and it is to the same source of authority that we must now refer.

Though I mean not to touch upon any sectarian principle of religion, yet it may be worth observing that the genealogy of Christ is traced to Adam. Why then not trace the rights of man to the creation of man? I will answer the question. Because there have been an upstart of governments, thrusting themselves between, and presumptuously working to *un-make* man.

If any generation of men ever possessed the right of dictating the mode by which the world should be governed forever, it was the first generation that existed; and if that generation did not do it, no succeeding generation can show any authority for doing it, nor set any up. The illuminating and divine principles of the equal rights of man (for it has its origin from the maker of man) relates, not only to the living individuals, but to generations of men succeeding each other. Every generation is equal in rights to the generations which preceded it, by the same rule that every individual is born equal in rights with his contemporary.

Every history of the creation, and every traditionary account, whether from the lettered or unlettered world, however they may vary in their opinion or belief of certain particulars, all agree in establishing one point, *the unity of man;* by which I mean that man is all of *one degree*, and consequently that all men are born equal and with equal natural rights, in the same manner as if posterity had been continued by *creation* instead of *generation*, the latter being only the mode by which the former is carried forward; and consequently every child born into the world must be considered as deriving its existence from God. The world is as new to him as it was to the first man that existed, and his natural right in it is of the same kind.

The Mosaic account of the creation, whether taken as divine authority, or merely historical, is fully up to this point, *the unity or equality of man.* The expressions admit of no controversy. "And God said, let us make man in our own image. In the image of God created he him; male and female created he them." The distinction of sexes is pointed out, but no other distinction is even implied. If this be not divine authority, it is at least historical authority, and shows that the equality of man, so far from being a modern doctrine, is the oldest upon record.

It is also to be observed that all the religions known in the world are founded, so far as they relate to man, on the *unity of man* as being all of one degree. Whether in heaven or in hell or in whatever state man may be supposed to exist hereafter, the good and the bad are the only distinctions. Nay, even the laws of governments are obliged to slide into this principle by making degrees to consist in crimes and not in persons.

It is one of the greatest of all truths, and of the highest advantage to cultivate. By considering man in this light, and by instructing him to consider himself in this light, it places him in a close connection with all his duties, whether to his creator, or to the creation of which he is a part; and it is only when he forgets his origin or, to use a more fashionable phrase, his *birth and family*, that he becomes dissolute. It is not among the least of the evils of the present existing governments in all parts of Europe, that man, considered as man, is thrown back to a vast distance from his maker, and the artificial chasm filled up by a succession of barriers, or a sort of turnpike gates, through which he has to pass. I will quote Mr. Burke's catalogue of barriers that he has set up between man and his maker. Putting himself in the character of a herald, he says, "We fear God—we look with *awe* to kings—with affection to parliaments—with duty to magistrates—with reverence to priests, and with respect to nobility." Mr. Burke has forgot to put in "chivalry." He has also forgot to put in Peter.

The duty of man is not a wilderness of turnpike gates through which he is to pass by tickets from one to the other. It is plain and simple, and consists but of two points. His duty to God, which every man must feel; and with respect to his neighbor, to do as he would be done by. If those to whom power is delegated do well, they will be respected; if not they will be despised; and with regard to those to whom no power is delegated, but who assume it, the rational world can know nothing of them.

Hitherto we have spoken only (and that but in part) of the natural rights of man. We have now to consider the civil rights of man, and to show how the one originates out of the other. Man did not enter into society to become *worse* than he was before, nor to have less rights than he had before, but to have those rights better secured. His natural rights are the foundation of all his civil rights. But in order to pursue this distinction with more precision, it is necessary to mark the different qualities of natural and civil rights.

A few words will explain this. Natural rights are those which always appertain to man in right of his existence. Of this kind are all the intellectual rights, or rights of the mind, and also all those rights of acting as an individual for his own comfort and happiness, which are not injurious to the rights of others. Civil rights are those which appertain to man in right of his being a member of society. Every civil right has for its foundation some natural right pre-existing in the individual, but to which his individual power is not, in all cases, sufficiently competent. Of this kind are all those which relate to security and protection.

From this short review, it will be easy to distinguish between that class of natural rights which man retains after entering into society and those which he throws into common stock as a member of society.

The natural rights which he retains are all those in which the power to execute is as perfect in the individual as the right itself. Among this class, as is before mentioned, are all the intellectual rights, or rights of the mind: consequently, religion is one of those rights. The natural rights which are not retained are all those in which, though the right is perfect in the individual, the power to execute them is defective. They answer not his purpose. A man, by natural right, has a right to judge in his own cause; and so far as the right of the mind is concerned, he never surrenders it: but what availeth it him to judge, if he has not power to redress? He therefore deposits this right in the common stock of society, and takes the arm of society, of which he is a part, in preference and in addition to his own. Society *grants* him nothing. Every man is a proprietor in society, and draws on the capital as a matter of right.

From these premises, two or three certain conclusions will follow.

1st, That every civil right grows out of a natural right; or, in other words, is a natural right exchanged.

2d, That civil power, properly considered as such, is made up of the aggregate of that class of the natural rights of man which becomes defective in the individual in point of power, and answers not his purpose, but when collected to a focus, becomes competent to the purpose of everyone.

3d, That the power produced by the aggregate of natural rights, imperfect in power in the individual, cannot be applied to invade the natural rights which are retained in the individual, and in which the power to execute is as perfect as the right itself.

We have now, in a few words, traced man from a natural individual to a member of society, and shown, or endeavored to show, the quality of the natural rights retained and of those which are exchanged for civil rights. Let us now apply those principles to government.

In casting our eyes over the world, it is extremely easy to distinguish the governments which have arisen out of society, or out of the social compact, from those which have not: but to place this in a clearer light than what a single glance may afford, it will be proper to take a review of the several sources from which governments have arisen and on which they have been founded.

They may be all comprehended under three heads: 1st, superstition; 2d, power; 3d, the common interests of society, and the common rights of man.

The first was a government of priestcraft, the second of conquerors, and the third of reason.

When a set of artful men pretended, through the medium of oracles, to hold intercourse with the deity as familiarly as they now march up the back stairs in European courts, the world was completely under the government of superstition. The oracles were consulted, and whatever they were made to say became the law; and this sort of government lasted just as long as this sort of superstition lasted.

After these a race of conquerors arose, whose government, like that of William the Conqueror, was founded in power, and the sword assumed the name of a scepter. Governments thus established last as long as the power to support them lasts; but that they might avail themselves of every engine in their favor, they united fraud to force, and set up an idol which they called *divine right*, and which, in imitation of the pope who affects to be spiritual and temporal, and in contradiction to the founder of the Christian religion, twisted itself afterwards into an idol of another shape, called *church and state*. The key of St. Peter and the key of the treasury became quartered on one another, and the wondering, cheated multitude, worshipped the invention.

When I contemplate the natural dignity of man; when I feel (for nature has not been kind enough to me to blunt my feelings) for the honor and happiness of its character, I become irritated at the attempt to govern mankind by force and fraud as if they were all knaves and fools, and can scarcely avoid feeling disgust for those who are thus imposed upon.

We have now to review the governments which arise out of society, in contradistinction to those which arose out of superstition and conquest.

It has been thought a considerable advance towards establishing the principles of freedom, to say that government is a compact between those who govern and those who are governed: but this cannot be true, because it is putting the effect before the cause; for as man must have existed before governments existed, there necessarily was a time when governments did not exist, and consequently there could originally exist no governors to form such a compact with. The fact therefore must be that the *individuals themselves*, each in his own personal and sovereign right, *entered into a compact with each other* to produce a government: and this is the only mode in which governments have a right to be established; and the only principle on which they have a right to exist.

To possess ourselves of a clear idea of what government is or ought to be, we must trace it to its origin. In doing this we shall easily discover that governments must have arisen, either *out* of the people, or *over* the people. Mr. Burke has made no distinction. He investigates nothing to its source, and therefore he confounds everything: but he has signified his intention of undertaking, at some future opportunity, a comparison between the constitutions of England and France. As he thus renders it a subject of controversy by throwing the gauntlet, I take him up on his own ground. It is in high challenges that high truths have the right of appearing; and I accept it with the more readiness, because it affords me, at the same time, an opportunity of pursuing the subject with respect to governments arising out of society.

But it will be first necessary to define what is meant by a *constitution*. It is not sufficient that we adopt the word; we must fix also a standard signification to it.

A constitution is not a thing in name only, but in fact. It has not an ideal, but a real existence; and wherever it cannot be produced in a visible form there is none. A constitution is a thing antecedent to a government, and a government is only the creature of a constitution. The constitution of a country is not the act of its government, but of the people constituting a government. It is the body of elements, to which you can refer, and quote article by article; and contains the principles on which the government shall be established, the form in which it shall be organized, the powers it shall have, the mode of elections, the duration of parliaments, or by what other name such bodies may be called; the powers which the executive part of the government shall have; and, in fine, everything that relates to the complete organization of a civil government, and the principle on which it shall act, and by which it shall be bound. A constitution, therefore, is to a government what the laws made afterwards by that government are to a court of judicature. The court of judicature does not make laws, neither can it alter them; it only acts in conformity to the laws made; and the government is in like manner governed by the constitution.

[THE ENGLISH AND FRENCH CONSTITUTIONS]

Can then Mr. Burke produce the English constitution? If he cannot, we may fairly conclude that though it has been so much talked about, no such thing as a constitution exists, or ever did exist, and consequently the people have yet a constitution to form.

Mr. Burke will not, I presume, deny the position I have already advanced; namely, that governments arise either *out* of the people, or *over* the people. The English government is one of those which arose out of a conquest, and not out of society, and consequently it arose over the people; and though it has been much modified from the opportunity of circumstances since the time of William the Conqueror, the country has never yet regenerated itself, and it is therefore without a constitution.

I readily perceive the reason why Mr. Burke declined going into the comparison between the English and the French constitutions, because he could not but perceive, when he sat down to the task, that no constitution was in existence on his side of the question. His book is certainly bulky enough to have contained all he could say on this subject, and it would have been the best manner in which people could have judged of their separate merits. Why then has he declined the only thing that was worth while to write upon? It was the strongest ground he could take if the advantages were on his side, but the weakest if they were not; and his declining to take it is either a sign that he could not possess it or could not maintain it.

Mr. Burke has said in his speech last winter in parliament, that when the national assembly of France first met in three orders (the *tiers états*, the clergy, and the *noblesse*), that France had then a good constitution. This shows, among numerous other instances, that Mr. Burke does not understand what a constitution is. The persons so met were not a *constitution*, but a *convention* to make a constitution.

The present national assembly of France is, strictly speaking, the personal social compact. The members of it are the delegates of the nation in its *original* character; future assemblies will be the delegates of the nation in its *organized* character. The authority of the present assembly is different to what the authority of future assemblies will be. The authority of the present one is to form a constitution: the authority of future assemblies will be to legislate according to the principles and forms prescribed in that constitution; and if experience should hereafter show that alterations, amendments, or additions are necessary, the constitution will point out the mode by which such things shall be done, and not leave it to the discretionary power of the future government.

A government on the principles on which constitutional governments, arising out of society, are established, cannot have the right of altering itself. If it had, it would be arbitrary. It might make itself what it pleased; and wherever such a right is set up, it shows that there is no constitution. The act by which the English parliament empowered itself to sit for seven years shows there is no constitution in England. It might, by the selfsame authority, have sat any greater number of years or for life. The bill which the present Mr. Pitt brought into parliament some years ago, to reform parliament, was on the same erroneous principle.

The right of reform is in the nation in its original character, and the constitutional method would be by a general convention elected for the purpose. There is moreover a paradox in the idea of vitiated bodies reforming themselves.

From these preliminaries I proceed to draw some comparisons. I have already spoken of the declaration of rights; and as I mean to be as concise as possible, I shall proceed to other parts of the French constitution.

The constitution of France says that every man who pays a tax of sixty sous per annum (2s. and 6d. English) is an elector. What article will Mr. Burke place against this? Can anything be more limited, and at the same time more capricious, than what the qualifications of electors are in England? Limited— because not one man in a hundred (I speak much within compass) is admitted to vote: capricious—because the lowest character that can be supposed to exist, and who has not so much as the visible means of an honest livelihood, is an elector in some places; while, in other places, the man who pays very large taxes, and with a fair known character, and the farmer who rents to the amount of three or four hundred pounds a year, and with a property on that farm to three or four times that amount, is not admitted to be an elector. Everything is out of nature, as Mr. Burke says on another occasion, in this strange chaos, and all sorts of follies are blended with all sorts of crimes. William the Conqueror and his descendants parcelled out the country in this manner, and bribed one part of it, by what they called charters, to hold the other parts of it the better subjected to their will. This is the reason why so many charters abound in Cornwall. The people were averse to the government established at the conquest, and the towns were garrisoned and bribed to enslave the country. All the old charters are the badges of this conquest, and it is from this source that the capriciousness of election arises.

The French constitution says that the number of representatives for any place shall be in a ratio to the number of taxable inhabitants or electors. What article will Mr. Burke place against this? The county of Yorkshire, which contains near a million of souls, sends two county members; and so does the county of Rutland, which contains not a hundredth part of that number. The town of old Sarum, which contains not three houses, sends two members; and the town of Manchester, which contains upwards of sixty thousand souls, is not admitted to send any. Is there any principle in these things? Is there anything by which you can trace the marks of freedom or discover those of wisdom? No wonder then Mr. Burke has declined the comparison, and endeavored to lead his readers from the point by a wild unsystematical display of paradoxical rhapsodies.

The French constitution says that the national assembly shall be elected every two years. What article will Mr. Burke place against this? Why, that the nation has no right at all in the case; that the government is perfectly arbitrary with respect to this point; and he can quote for his authority the precedent of a former parliament.

The French constitution says there shall be no game laws; that the farmer on whose land wild game shall be found (for it is by the produce of those lands they are fed) shall have a right to what he can take. That there shall be no monopolies of any kind, that all trades shall be free, and every man free to follow any occupation by which he can procure an honest livelihood, and in any place, town, or city, throughout the nation. What will Mr. Burke say to this? In England game is made the property of those at whose expense it is not fed; and with respect to monopolies, the country is cut up into monopolies. Every chartered town is an aristocratic monopoly in itself, and the qualification of electors proceeds out of those chartered monopolies. Is this freedom? Is this what Mr. Burke means by a constitution?

In these chartered monopolies a man coming from another part of the country is hunted from them as if he were a foreign enemy. An Englishman is not free in his own country; every

one of those places presents a barrier in his way, and tells him
he is not a freeman—that he has no rights. Within these
monopolies are other monopolies. In a city, such for instance
as Bath, which contains between twenty and thirty thousand
inhabitants, the right of electing representatives to parliament
is monopolized into about thirty-one persons. And within
these monopolies are still others. A man, even of the same
town, whose parents were not in circumstances to give him an
occupation, is debarred in many cases from the natural right of
acquiring one, be his genius or industry what it may.

Are these things examples to hold out to a country regenerating itself from slavery, like France? Certainly they are not;
and certain am I that when the people of England come to reflect upon them, they will, like France, annihilate those badges
of ancient oppression, those traces of a conquered nation. Had
Mr. Burke possessed talents similar to the author of *On the
Wealth of Nations*, he would have comprehended all the parts
which enter into, and, by assemblage, form a constitution. He
would have reasoned from minutiæ to magnitude. It is not
from his prejudices only, but from the disorderly cast of his
genius, that he is unfitted for the subject he writes upon. Even
his genius is without a constitution. It is a genius at random,
and not a genius constituted. But he must say something. He
has therefore mounted in the air like a balloon to draw the eyes
of the multitude from the ground they stand upon.

Much is to be learned from the French constitution. Conquest and tyranny transplanted themselves with William the
Conqueror from Normandy into England, and the country is
yet disfigured with the marks. May then the example of all
France contribute to regenerate the freedom which a province
of it destroyed!

The French constitution says that to preserve the national
representation from being corrupt no member of the national
assembly shall be an officer of government, a placeman, or a
pensioner. What will Mr. Burke place against this? I will
whisper his answer: *loaves* and *fishes*. Ah! this government of
loaves and fishes has more mischief in it than people have yet

reflected on. The national assembly has made the discovery, and holds out an example to the world. Had governments agreed to quarrel on purpose to fleece their countries by taxes, they could not have succeeded better than they have done.

Everything in the English government appears to me the reverse of what it ought to be, and of what it is said to be. The parliament, imperfectly and capriciously elected as it is, is nevertheless *supposed* to hold the national purse in *trust* for the nation; but in the manner in which an English parliament is constructed, it is like a man being both mortgager and mortgagee; and in the case of misapplication of trust, it is the criminal sitting in judgment on himself. If those persons who vote the supplies are the same persons who receive the supplies when voted, and are to account for the expenditure of those supplies to those who voted them, it is *themselves accountable to themselves*, and the Comedy of Errors concludes with the pantomime of *Hush*. Neither the ministerial party nor the opposition will touch upon this case. The national purse is the common hack which each mounts upon. It is like what the country people call, "Ride and tie—You ride a little way and then I." They order these things better in France.

The French constitution says that the right of war and peace is in the nation. Where else should it reside but in those who are to pay the expense?

In England the right is said to reside in a *metaphor*, shown at the tower for sixpence or a shilling apiece; so are the lions; and it would be a step nearer to reason to say it resided in them, for any inanimate metaphor is no more than a hat or a cap. We can all see the absurdity of worshipping Aaron's molten calf, or Nebuchadnezzar's golden image; but why do men continue to practice on themselves the absurdities they despise in others?

It may with reason be said that in the manner the English nation is represented it matters not where this right resides, whether in the crown or in the parliament. War is the common harvest of all those who participate in the division and expenditure of public money in all countries. It is the art of *conquering at home:* the object of it is an increase of revenue; and as revenue cannot be increased without taxes, a pretense must be made for expenditures. In reviewing the history of the English government, its wars and taxes, an observer, not blinded by prejudice nor warped by interest, would declare that taxes were not raised to carry on wars, but that wars were raised to carry on taxes.

Mr. Burke, as a member of the house of commons, is a part of the English government; and though he professes himself an enemy to war, he abuses the French constitution, which seeks to explode it. He holds up the English government as a model in all its parts to France; but he should first know the remarks which the French make upon it. They contend, in favor of their own, that the portion of liberty enjoyed in England is just enough to enslave a country by, more productively than by despotism; and that as the real object of a despotism is revenue, a government so formed obtains more than it could either by direct despotism or in a full state of freedom, and is, therefore, on the ground of interest, opposed to both. They account also for the readiness which always appears in such governments for engaging in wars by remarking on the different motives which produce them. In despotic governments, wars are the effects of pride; but in those governments in which they become the means of taxation, they acquire thereby a more permanent promptitude.

The French constitution, therefore, to provide against both those evils, has taken away from kings and ministers the power of declaring war, and placed the right where the expense must fall.

When the question on the right of war and peace was agitating in the national assembly, the people of England appeared to be much interested in the event, and highly to applaud the decision. As a principle it applies as much to one country as to another. William the Conqueror, *as a conqueror*, held this power of war and peace in himself, and his descendants have ever since claimed it as a right.

Although Mr. Burke has asserted the right of the parliament

at the revolution to bind and control the nation and posterity *forever*, he denies at the same time that the parliament or the nation had any right to alter what he calls the succession of the crown, in anything but in part, or by a sort of modification. By his taking this ground he throws the case back to the *Norman Conquest;* and by thus running a line of succession, springing from William the Conqueror to the present day, he makes it necessary to inquire who and what William the Conqueror was, and where he came from; and into the origin, history, and nature of what are called prerogatives. Everything must have had a beginning, and the fog of time and of antiquity should be penetrated to discover it. Let then Mr. Burke bring forward his William of Normandy, for it is to this origin that his argument goes. It also unfortunately happens in running this line of succession, that another line, parallel thereto, presents itself, which is, that if the succession runs in a line of the conquest, the nation runs in a line of being conquered, and it ought to rescue itself from this reproach.

But it will perhaps be said that though the power of declaring war descends into the heritage of the conquest, it is held in check by the right of the parliament to withhold the supplies. It will always happen when a thing is originally wrong that amendments do not make it right, and it often happens that they do as much mischief one way as good the other: and such is the case here, for if the one rashly declares war as a matter of right, and the other peremptorily withholds the supplies as a matter of right, the remedy becomes as bad or worse than the disease. The one forces the nation to a combat, and the other ties its hands; but the more probable issue is that the contrast will end in a collusion between the parties, and be made a screen to both.

On this question of war, three things are to be considered; 1st, the right of declaring it; 2d, the expense of supporting it; 3d, the mode of conducting it after it is declared. The French constitution places the *right* where the *expense* must fall, and this union can be only in the nation. The mode of conducting it, after it is declared, it consigns to the executive department.

Were this the case in all countries, we should hear but little more of wars.

Before I proceed to consider other parts of the French constitution, and by way of relieving the fatigue of argument, I will introduce an anecdote which I had from Dr. Franklin.

While the doctor resided in France, as minister from America during the war, he had numerous proposals made to him by projectors of every country and of every kind, who wished to go to the land that floweth with milk and honey, America; and among the rest there was one who offered himself to be king. He introduced his proposal to the doctor by letter, which is now in the hands of M. Beaumarchais, of Paris—stating, first, that as the Americans had dismissed or sent away their king, they would want another. Secondly, that himself was a Norman. Thirdly, that he was of a more ancient family than the dukes of Normandy, and of a more honorable descent, his line having never been bastardized. Fourthly, that there was already a precedent in England of kings coming out of Normandy; and on these grounds he rested his offer, *enjoining* that the doctor would forward it to America. But as the doctor did not do this, nor yet send him an answer, the projector wrote a second letter; in which he did not, it is true, threaten to go over and conquer America, but only, with great dignity, proposed that if his offer was not accepted, that an acknowledgment of about £30,000 might be made to him for his generosity! Now, as all arguments respecting succession must necessarily connect that succession with some beginning, Mr. Burke's arguments on this subject go to show that there is no English origin of kings, and that they are descendants of the Norman line in right of the conquest. It may, therefore, be of service to his doctrine to make the story known, and to inform him that, in case of that natural extinction to which all mortality is subject, kings may again be had from Normandy on more reasonable terms than William the Conqueror; and, consequently, that the good people of England at the revolution of 1688 might have done much better had such a generous Norman as *this* known *their* wants, and they *his*. The chivalric character which Mr.

Burke so much admires is certainly much easier to make a bargain with than a hard-dealing Dutchman. But to return to the
matters of the constitution.

The French constitution says *there shall be no titles;* and of
consequence all that class of equivocal generation which in
some countries is called "*aristocracy*," and in others "*nobility*,"
is done away, and the *peer* is exalted into the *man.*

Titles are but nicknames, and every nickname is a title. The
thing is perfectly harmless in itself, but it marks a sort of
foppery in the human character which degrades it. It renders
man diminutive in things which are great, and the counterfeit of woman in things which are little. It talks about its
fine *riband* like a girl, and shows its *garter* like a child. A
certain writer, of some antiquity, says, "When I was a child, I
thought as a child; but when I became a man, I put away childish
things."

It is, properly, from the elevated mind of France that the
folly of titles has been abolished. It has outgrown the baby-
clothes of *count* and *duke*, and breeched itself in manhood.
France has not levelled, it has exalted. It has put down the
dwarf to set up the man. The insignificance of a senseless word
like *duke*, *count*, or *earl*, has ceased to please. Even those who
possessed them have disowned the gibberish and, as they out-
grew the rickets, have despised the rattle. The genuine mind
of man, thirsting for its native home, society, contemns the
gewgaws that separate him from it. Titles are like circles
drawn by the magician's wand to contract the sphere of man's
felicity. He lives immured within the Bastile of a word, and
surveys at a distance the envied life of man.

Is it then any wonder that titles should fall in France? Is
it not a greater wonder they should be kept up anywhere?
What are they? What is their worth, nay "what is their
amount?" When we think or speak of a *judge*, or a *general*,
we associate with it the ideas of office and character; we think
of gravity in the one, and bravery in the other; but when we
use a word merely as a title, no ideas associate with it. Through
all the vocabulary of Adam, there is not such an animal as a

duke or a count; neither can we connect any certain idea to the words. Whether they mean strength or weakness, wisdom or folly, a child or a man, or a rider or a horse, is all equivocal. What respect then can be paid to that which describes nothing, and which means nothing? Imagination has given figure and character to centaurs, satyrs, and down to all the fairy tribe; but titles baffle even the powers of fancy, and are a chimerical nondescript.

But this is not all. If a whole country is disposed to hold them in contempt, all their value is gone, and none will own them. It is common opinion only that makes them anything or nothing, or worse than nothing. There is no occasion to take titles away, for they take themselves away when society concurs to ridicule them. This species of imaginary consequence has visibly declined in every part of Europe, and it hastens to its exit as the world of reason continues to rise. There was a time when the lowest class of what are called nobility was more thought of than the highest is now, and when a man in armor riding through Christendom in search of adventures was more stared at than a modern duke. The world has seen this folly fall, and it has fallen by being laughed at, and the farce of titles will follow its fate. The patriots of France have discovered in good time that rank and dignity in society must take a new ground. The old one has fallen through. It must now take the substantial ground of character instead of the chimerical ground of titles; and they have brought their titles to the altar, and made of them a burnt offering to reason.

If no mischief had annexed itself to the folly of titles, they would not have been worth a serious and formal destruction, such as the national assembly have decreed them; and this makes it necessary to inquire further into the nature and character of aristocracy.

That, then, which is called aristocracy in some countries, and nobility in others, arose out of the governments founded upon conquest. It was originally a military order for the purpose of supporting military government (for such were all governments founded in conquests); and to keep up a succession of this order for the purpose for which it was established, all the younger branches of those families were disinherited, and the law of *primogenitureship* set up.

The nature and character of aristocracy shows itself to us in this law. It is a law against every law of nature, and nature herself calls for its destruction. Establish family justice and aristocracy falls. By the aristocratical law of primogenitureship, in a family of six children, five are exposed. Aristocracy has never but *one* child. The rest are begotten to be devoured. They are thrown to the cannibal for prey, and the natural parent prepares the unnatural repast.

As everything which is out of nature in man affects, more or less, the interest of society, so does this. All the children which the aristocracy disowns (which are all, except the eldest) are, in general, cast like orphans on a parish, to be provided for by the public, but at a greater charge. Unnecessary offices and places in governments and courts are created at the expense of the public to maintain them.

With what kind of parental reflections can the father or mother contemplate their younger offspring. By nature they are children, and by marriage they are heirs; but by aristocracy they are bastards and orphans. They are the flesh and blood of their parents in one line, and nothing akin to them in the other. To restore, therefore, parents to their children, and children to their parents—relations to each other, and man to society—and to exterminate the monster aristocracy, root and branch—the French constitution has destroyed the law of *primogenitureship*. Here then lies the monster, and Mr. Burke, if he pleases, may write its epitaph.

Hitherto we have considered aristocracy chiefly in one point of view. We have now to consider it in another. But whether we view it before or behind, or sideways, or any way else, domestically or publicly, it is still a monster.

In France aristocracy had one feature less in its countenance than what it has in some other countries. It did not compose a body of hereditary legislators. It was not *"a corporation of aristocracy*," for such I have heard M. de la Fayette describe an English house of peers. Let us then examine the grounds upon which the French constitution has resolved against having such a house in France.

Because, in the first place, as is already mentioned, aristocracy is kept up by family tyranny and injustice.

2nd, Because there is an unnatural unfitness in an aristocracy to be legislators for a nation. Their ideas of *distributive justice* are corrupted at the very source. They begin life trampling on all their younger brothers and sisters, and relations of every kind, and are taught and educated so to do. With what ideas of justice or honor can that man enter a house of legislation, who absorbs in his own person the inheritance of a whole family of children, or metes out some pitiful portion with the insolence of a gift?

3d, Because the idea of hereditary legislators is as inconsistent as that of hereditary judges, or hereditary juries; and as absurd as an hereditary mathematician, or an hereditary wise man; and as ridiculous as an hereditary poet laureate.

4th, Because a body of men, holding themselves accountable to nobody, ought not to be trusted by anybody.

5th, Because it is continuing the uncivilized principle of governments founded in conquest, and the base idea of man having property in man and governing him by personal right.

6th, Because aristocracy has a tendency to degenerate the human species. By the universal economy of nature it is known, and by the instance of the Jews it is proved, that the human species has a tendency to degenerate, in any small number of persons, when separated from the general stock of society, and intermarrying constantly with each other. It defeats even its pretended end, and becomes in time the opposite of what is noble in man. Mr. Burke talks of nobility; let him show what it is. The greatest characters the world has known have rose on the democratic floor. Aristocracy has not been able to keep a proportionate pace with democracy. The artificial *noble* shrinks into a dwarf before the *noble* of nature; and in the few instances (for there are some in all countries) in whom nature, as by a miracle, has survived in aristocracy, *those men despise it.* But it is time to proceed to a new subject.

The French constitution has reformed the condition of the clergy. It has raised the income of the lower and middle classes, and taken from the higher. None are now less than twelve hundred livres (fifty pounds sterling), nor any higher than two or three thousand pounds. What will Mr. Burke place against this? Hear what he says.

He says that "the people of England can see, without pain or grudging, an archbishop precede a duke; they can see a bishop of Durham, or a bishop of Winchester, in possession of £10,000 a year; and cannot see why it is in worse hands than estates to the like amount in the hands of this earl or that 'squire." And Mr. Burke offers this as an example to France.

As to the first part, whether the archbishop precedes the duke, or the duke the bishop, it is, I believe, to the people in general, somewhat like *Sternhold* and *Hopkins,* or *Hopkins* and *Sternhold;* you may put which you please first: and as I confess that I do not understand the merits of this case, I will not contend it with Mr. Burke.

But with respect to the latter, I have something to say. Mr. Burke has not put the case right. The comparison is out of order by being put between the bishop and the earl or the 'squire. It ought to be put between the bishop and the curate, and then it will stand thus: *the people of England can see without grudging or pain, a bishop of Durham or a bishop of Winchester, in possession of ten thousand pounds a year, and a curate on thirty or forty pounds a year, or less.* No, sir, they certainly do not see these things without great pain and grudging. It is a case that applies itself to every man's sense of justice, and is one among many that calls aloud for a constitution.

In France the cry of *"the church! the church!"* was repeated as often as in Mr. Burke's book, and as loudly as when the dissenters' bill was before parliament; but the generality of the French clergy were not to be deceived by this cry any longer. They knew that whatever the pretense might be, it was themselves who were one of the principal objects of it. It was the cry of the high beneficed clergy to prevent any regulation of income taking place between those of ten thousand pounds a year and the parish priest. They, therefore, joined their case to those of every other oppressed class of men, and by this union obtained redress.

The French constitution has abolished tithes, that source of perpetual discontent between the tithe-holder and the parishioner. When land is held on tithe, it is in the condition of an estate held between two parties; one receiving one tenth, and the other nine tenths of the produce; and, consequently, on principles of equity, if the estate can be improved and made to produce by that improvement double or treble what it did before, or in any other ratio, the expense of such improvement ought to be borne in like proportion between the parties who are to share the produce. But this is not the case in tithes; the farmer bears the whole expense, and the tithe-holder takes a tenth of the improvement, in addition to the original tenth, and by this means gets the value of two tenths instead of one. This is another case that calls for a constitution.

The French constitution hath abolished or renounced *toleration*, and *intoleration* also, and hath established *universal right of conscience*.

Toleration is not the *opposite* of intoleration, but is the *counterfeit* of it. Both are despotisms. The one assumes to itself the right of withholding liberty of conscience, and the other of granting it. The one is the pope, armed with fire and faggot, and the other is the pope selling or granting indulgences. The former is church and state, and the latter is church and traffic.

But toleration may be viewed in a much stronger light. Man worships not himself, but his maker; and the liberty of conscience which he claims is not for the service of himself, but of his God. In this case, therefore, we must necessarily have the associated idea of two beings; the *mortal* who renders the worship, and the *immortal being* who is worshipped. Toleration therefore places itself not between man and man, nor between church and church, nor between one denomination of religion and another, but between God and man; between the being who worships, and the *being* who is worshipped; and by the same act of assumed authority by which it tolerates man to pay his worship, it presumptuously and blasphemously sets up itself to tolerate the Almighty to receive it.

Were a bill brought into parliament, entitled, "An *act* to tolerate or grant liberty to the Almighty to receive the worship of a Jew or a Turk," or "to prohibit the Almighty from receiving it," all men would startle, and call it blasphemy. There would be an uproar. The presumption of toleration in religious matters would then present itself unmasked; but the presumption is not the less because the name of "man" only appears to those laws, for the associated idea of the *worshipper* and the *worshipped* cannot be separated. Who, then, art thou, vain dust and ashes! by whatever name thou art called, whether a king, a bishop, a church or a state, a parliament or anything else, that obtrudest thine insignificance between the soul of man and his maker? Mind thine own concerns. If he believes not as thou believest, it is a proof that thou believest not as he believeth, and there is no earthly power can determine between you.

With respect to what are called denominations of religion, if everyone is left to judge of his own religion, there is no such thing as a religion that is wrong; but if they are to judge of each other's religion, there is no such thing as a religion that is right; and therefore all the world is right, or all the world is wrong. But with respect to religion itself, without regard to names, and as directing itself from the universal family of mankind to the divine object of all adoration, *it is man bringing to his maker the fruits of his heart;* and though these fruits may differ from each other like the fruits of the earth, the grateful tribute of everyone is accepted.

A bishop of Durham, or a bishop of Winchester, or the archbishop who heads the dukes, will not refuse a tithe-sheaf of wheat, because it is not a cock of hay; nor a cock of hay, because it is not a sheaf of wheat; nor a pig because it is neither the one nor the other: but these same persons, under the figure

of an established church, will not permit their maker to receive
the varied tithes of man's devotion.

One of the continual choruses of Mr. Burke's book is "church
and state"; he does not mean some one particular church, or
some one particular state, but any church and state; and he uses
the term as a general figure to hold forth the political doctrine
of always uniting the church with the state in every country,
and he censures the national assembly for not having done this
in France. Let us bestow a few thoughts on this subject.

All religions are in their nature mild and benign, and united
with principles of morality. They could not have made prose-
lytes at first by professing anything that was vicious, cruel, per-
secuting, or immoral. Like everything else, they had their
beginning; and they proceeded by persuasion, exhortation, and
example. How then is it that they lose their native mildness,
and become morose and intolerant?

It proceeds from the connection which Mr. Burke recom-
mends. By engendering the church with the state, a sort of
mule animal, capable only of destroying and not of breeding
up, is produced, called *the church established by law*. It is a
stranger, even from its birth, to any parent mother on which it
is begotten, and whom in time it kicks out and destroys.

The inquisition in Spain does not proceed from the religion
originally professed, but from this mule animal, engendered
between the church and the state. The burnings in Smithfield
proceeded from the same heterogeneous production; and it was
regeneration of this strange animal in England afterwards that
renewed rancor and irreligion among the inhabitants, and that
drove the people called Quakers and Dissenters to America.
Persecution is not an original feature in *any* religion; but it is
always the strongly-marked feature of all law-religions, or
religions established by law. Take away the law-establishment,
and every religion reassumes its original benignity. In America, a catholic priest is a good citizen, a good character, and a
good neighbor; an episcopalian minister is of the same description: and this proceeds, independent of men, from there being
no law-establishment in America.

If also we view this matter in a temporal sense, we shall see the ill effects it has had on the prosperity of nations. The union of church and state has impoverished Spain. The revoking the edict of Nantz drove the silk manufacture from that country into England; and church and state are now driving the cotton manufacture from England to America and France. Let then Mr. Burke continue to preach his antipolitical doctrine of church and state. It will do some good. The national assembly will not follow his advice, but will benefit by his folly. It was by observing the ill effects of it in England, that America has been warned against it; and it is by experiencing them in France, that the national assembly have abolished it, and, like America, has established *universal right of conscience, and universal right of citizenship.*[1]

[1] When in any country we see extraordinary circumstances taking place, they naturally lead any man who has a talent for observation and investigation to inquire into the causes. The manufacturers of Manchester, Birmingham, and Sheffield are the principal manufacturers in England. From whence did this arise? A little observation will explain the case. The principal, and the generality of the inhabitants of those places, are not of what is called in England the church established by law: and they, or their fathers (for it is within but a few years) withdrew from the persecution of the chartered towns, where test-laws more particularly operate, and established a sort of asylum for themselves in those places. It was the only asylum then offered, for the rest of Europe was worse. But the case is now changing. France and America bid all comers welcome, and initiate them into all the rights of citizenship. Policy and interest, therefore, will, but perhaps too late, dictate in England what reason and justice could not. Those manufacturers are withdrawing to other places. There is now erecting in Passey, three miles from Paris, a large cotton manufactory, and several are already erected in America. Soon after the rejecting the bill for repealing the test-law, one of the richest manufacturers in England said in my hearing, "England, sir, is not a country for a Dissenter to live in,—we must go to France." These are truths, and it is doing justice to both parties to tell them. It is chiefly the Dissenters that have carried English manufactures to the height they are now at, and the same men have it in their power to carry them away; and though those manufactures would afterwards continue in those places, the foreign market will be lost. There frequently appears in the London Gazette extracts from certain acts to prevent machines, and as far as it can extend to persons, from going

I will here cease the comparison with respect to the principles of the French constitution, and conclude this part of the subject with a few observations on the organization of the formal parts of the French and English governments.

The executive power in each country is in the hands of a person styled the king; but the French constitution distinguishes between the king and the sovereign: it considers the station of king as official, and places sovereignty in the nation.

The representatives of the nation, which compose the national assembly and who are the legislative power, originate in and from the people by election, as an inherent right in the people. In England it is otherwise; and this arises from the original establishment of what is called its monarchy; for as by the conquest all the rights of the people or the nation were absorbed into the hands of the conqueror, and who added the title of king to that of conqueror, those same matters which in France are now held as rights in the people, or in the nation, are held in England as grants from what is called the crown. The parliament in England, in both its branches, was erected by patents from the descendants of the conqueror. The house of commons did not originate as a matter of right in the people, to delegate or elect, but as a grant or boon.

By the French constitution the nation is always named before the king. The third article of the declaration of rights says, *"The nation is essentially the source* (or fountain) *of all sovereignty."* Mr. Burke argues that in England a king is the fountain—that he is the fountain of all honor. But as this idea is evidently descended from the conquest, I shall make no other remark upon it than that it is the nature of conquest to turn everything upside down; and as Mr. Burke will not be refused

---

out of the country. It appears from these that the ill effects of the test-laws and church-establishment begin to be much suspected; but the remedy of force can never supply the remedy of reason. In the progress of less than a century, all the unrepresented part of England, of all denominations which is at least an hundred times the most numerous, may begin to feel the necessity of a constitution, and then all those matters will come regularly before them.

the privilege of speaking twice, and as there are but two parts in the figure, the *fountain* and the *spout*, he will be right the second time.

The French constitution puts the legislative before the executive; the law before the king; *la loi, le roi*. This also is in the natural order of things; because laws must have existence before they can have execution.

A king in France does not, in addressing himself to the national assembly, say "my assembly," similar to the phrase used in England of "*my* parliament"; neither can he use it consistent with the constitution, nor could it be admitted. There may be propriety in the use of it in England, because, as is before mentioned, both houses of parliament originated out of what is called the crown, by patent or boon—and not out of the inherent rights of the people as the national assembly does in France, and whose name designates its origin.

The president of the national assembly does not ask the king *to grant to the assembly the liberty of speech*, as is the case with the English house of commons. The constitutional dignity of the national assembly cannot debase itself. Speech is, in the first place, one of the natural rights of man, always retained; and with respect to the national assembly, the use of it is their *duty*, and the nation is their *authority*. They were elected by the greatest body of men exercising the right of election the European world ever saw. They sprung not from the filth of rotten boroughs, nor are they vassal representatives of aristocratical ones. Feeling the proper dignity of their character, they support it. Their parliamentary language, whether for or against a question, is free, bold, and manly, and extends to all the parts and circumstances of the case. If any matter or subject respecting the executive department or the person who presides in it (the king) comes before them, it is debated on with the spirit of men and the language of gentlemen; and their answer, or their address, is returned in the same style. They stand not aloft with the gaping vacuity of vulgar ignorance, nor bend with the cringe of sycophantic insignificance. The graceful pride of truth knows no extremes, and preserves in every latitude of life the right-angled character of man.

Let us now look to the other side of the question. In the addresses of the English parliaments to their kings, we see neither the intrepid spirit of the old parliaments of France, nor the serene dignity of the present national assembly; neither do we see in them anything of the style of English manners, which borders somewhat on bluntness. Since then they are neither of foreign extraction, nor naturally of English production, their origin must be sought for elsewhere, and that origin is the Norman Conquest. They are evidently of the vassalage class of manners, and emphatically mark the prostrate distance that exists in no other condition of men than between the conqueror and the conquered. That this vassalage idea and style of speaking was not got rid of, even at the revolution of 1688, is evident from the declaration of parliament to William and Mary, in these words: "We do most humbly and faithfully *submit* ourselves, our heirs and posterity forever." Submission is wholly a vassalage term, repugnant to the dignity of freedom, and an echo of the language used at the conquest.

As the estimation of all things is by comparison, the revolution of 1688, however from circumstances it may have been exalted above its value, will find its level. It is already on the wane, eclipsed by the enlarging orb of reason, and the revolutions of America and France. In less than another century it will go, as well as Mr. Burke's labors, "to the family vault of all the Capulets." Mankind will then scarcely believe that a country calling itself free would send to Holland for a man, and clothe him with power, on purpose to put themselves in fear of him, and give him almost a million sterling a year for leave to *submit* themselves and their posterity, like bondmen and bondwomen forever.

But there is a truth that ought to be made known; I have had the opportunity of seeing it: which is *that, notwithstanding appearances, there is not any description of men that despise monarchy so much as courtiers.* But they well know that if it were seen by others, as it is seen by them, the juggle could not be kept up. They are in the condition of men who get their living by show, and to whom the folly of that show is so familiar that they ridicule it; but were the audience to be made as wise in this respect as themselves, there would be an end to the show and the profits with it. The difference between a republican and a courtier with respect to monarchy is that the one opposes monarchy believing it to be something, and the other laughs at it knowing it to be nothing.

As I used sometimes to correspond with Mr. Burke, believing him then to be a man of sounder principles than his book shows him to be, I wrote to him last winter from Paris and gave him an account how prosperously matters were going on. Among other subjects in that letter, I referred to the happy situation the national assembly were placed in; that they had taken a ground on which their moral duty and their political interest were united. They have not to hold out a language which they do not believe, for the fraudulent purpose of making others believe it. Their station requires no artifice to support it, and can only be maintained by enlightening mankind. It is not their interest to cherish ignorance, but to dispel it. They are not in the case of a ministerial or an opposition party in England, who, though they are opposed, are still united to keep up the common mystery. The national assembly must throw open a magazine of light. It must show man the proper character of man; and the nearer it can bring him to that standard, the stronger the national assembly becomes.

In contemplating the French constitution, we see in it a rational order of things. The principles harmonize with the forms, and both with their origin. It may perhaps be said as an excuse for bad forms, that they are nothing more than forms; but this is a mistake. Forms grow out of principles, and operate to continue the principles they grow from. It is impossible to practice a bad form on anything but a bad principle. It cannot be ingrafted on a good one; and wherever the forms in any government are bad, it is a certain indication that the principles are bad also.

I will here finally close this subject. I began it by remarking that Mr. Burke had *voluntarily* declined going into a comparison of the English and French constitutions. He apologizes for not doing it by saying that he had not time. Mr. Burke's book was upwards of eight months in hand, and it extended to a volume of three hundred and fifty-six pages. As his omission does injury to his cause, his apology makes it worse; and men on the English side of the water will begin to consider whether there is not some radical defect in what is called the English constitution that made it necessary in Mr. Burke to suppress the comparison, to avoid bringing it into view.

[STEPS LEADING TO THE REVOLUTION]

As Mr. Burke has not written on constitutions, so neither has he written on the French revolution. He gives no account of its commencement or its progress. He only expresses his wonder. "It looks," says he, "to me as if I were in a great crisis, not of the affairs of France alone, but of all Europe, perhaps of more than Europe. All circumstances taken together, the French revolution is the most astonishing that has hitherto happened in the world."

As wise men are astonished at foolish things, and other people at wise ones, I know not on which ground to account for Mr. Burke's astonishment; but certain it is that he does not understand the French revolution. It has apparently burst forth like a creation from a chaos, but it is no more than the consequence of mental revolution previously existing in France. The mind of the nation had changed beforehand, and a new order of things has naturally followed a new order of thoughts. I will here, as concisely as I can, trace out the growth of the French revolution, and mark the circumstances that have contributed to produce it.

The despotism of Louis XIV, united with the gaiety of his court and the gaudy ostentation of his character, had so humbled, and at the same time so fascinated the mind of France, that the people appear to have lost all sense of their own dignity in contemplating that of their grand monarch; and the whole reign of Louis XV, remarkable only for weakness and effeminacy, made no other alteration than that of spreading a sort of lethargy over the nation, from which it showed no disposition to rise.

The only signs which appeared of the spirit of liberty during those periods are to be found in the writings of the French philosophers. Montesquieu, president of the parliament of Bordeaux, went as far as a writer under a despotic government could well proceed; and being obliged to divide himself between principle and prudence, his mind often appears under a veil, and we ought to give him credit for more than he has expressed.

Voltaire, who was both the flatterer and satirist of despotism, took another line. His forte lay in exposing and ridiculing the superstitions which priestcraft, united with statecraft, had interwoven with governments. It was not from the purity of his principles, or his love of mankind (for satire and philanthropy are not naturally concordant), but from his strong capacity of seeing folly in its true shape and his irresistible propensity to expose it, that he made those attacks. They were however as formidable as if the motives had been virtuous; and he merits the thanks rather than the esteem of mankind.

On the contrary we find in the writings of Rousseau and Abbé Raynal a loveliness of sentiment in favor of liberty that excites respect and elevates the human faculties; yet having raised this animation, they do not direct its operations, but leave the mind in love with an object, without describing the means of possessing it.

The writings of Quisne, Turgot, and the friends of those authors are of a serious kind; but they labored under the same disadvantage with Montesquieu; their writings abound with moral maxims of government, but are rather directed to economize and reform the administration of the government than the government itself.

But all those writings and many others had their weight; and by the different manner in which they treated the subject of government—Montesquieu by his judgment and knowledge of laws, Voltaire by his wit, Rousseau and Raynal by their animation, and Quisne and Turgot by their moral maxims and systems of economy—readers of every class met with something to their taste, and a spirit of political inquiry began to diffuse itself through the nation at the time the dispute between England and the then colonies of America broke out.

In the war which France afterwards engaged in, it is very well known that the nation appeared to be beforehand with the French ministry. Each of them had its views; but those views were directed to different objects; the one sought liberty and the other retaliation on England. The French officers and soldiers who after this went to America were eventually placed in the school of freedom, and learned the practice as well as the principles of it by heart.

As it was impossible to separate the military events which took place in America from the principles of the American revolution, the publication of those events in France necessarily connected themselves with the principles that produced them. Many of the facts were in themselves principles; such as the declaration of American Independence, and the treaty of alliance between France and America, which recognized the natural rights of man and justified resistance to oppression.

The then minister of France, Count Vergennes, was not the friend of America; and it is both justice and gratitude to say that it was the queen of France who gave the cause of America a fashion at the French court. Count Vergennes was the personal and social friend of Dr. Franklin; and the doctor had obtained by his sensible gracefulness a sort of influence over him; but with respect to principles, Count Vergennes was a despot.

The situation of Dr. Franklin as minister from America to France should be taken into the chain of circumstances. A diplomatic character is the narrowest sphere of society that man can act in. It forbids intercourse by a reciprocity of suspicion; and a diplomatist is a sort of unconnected atom, continually repelling and repelled. But this was not the case with Dr. Franklin; he was not the diplomatist of a court, but of *man*.

His character as a philosopher had been long established, and his circle of society in France was universal.

Count Vergennes resisted for a considerable time the publication of the American constitutions in France, translated into the French language; but even in this he was obliged to give way to public opinion, and a sort of propriety in admitting to appear what he had undertaken to defend. The American constitutions were to liberty what a grammar is to language: they define its parts of speech, and practically construct them into syntax.

The peculiar situation of the then Marquis de la Fayette is another link in the great chain. He served in America as an American officer, under a commission of congress, and by the universality of his acquaintance was in close friendship with the civil government of America as well as with the military line. He spoke the language of the country, entered into the discussions on the principles of government, and was always a welcome friend at any election.

When the war closed, a vast reinforcement to the cause of liberty spread itself over France, by the return of the French officers and soldiers. A knowledge of the practice was then joined to the theory; and all that was wanting to give it real existence was opportunity. Man cannot, properly speaking, make circumstances for his purpose, but he always has it in his power to improve them when they occur; and this was the case in France.

M. Neckar was displaced in May, 1781; and by the ill management of the finances afterwards, and particularly during the extravagant administration of M. Calonne, the revenue of France which was nearly twenty-four millions sterling per year, was become unequal to the expenditures, not because the revenue had decreased, but because the expenses had increased, and this was the circumstance which the nation laid hold of to bring forward a revolution. The English minister, Mr. Pitt, has frequently alluded to the state of the French finances in his budgets, without understanding the subject. Had the French parliaments been as ready to register edicts for new taxes as an

English parliament is to grant them, there had been no derangement in the finances, nor yet any revolution; but this will better explain itself as I proceed.

It will be necessary here to show how taxes were formerly raised in France. The king, or rather the court or ministry, acting under the use of that name, framed the edicts for taxes at their own discretion and sent them to the parliaments to be registered; for until they were registered by the parliaments, they were not operative. Disputes had long existed between the court and the parliament with respect to the extent of the parliament's authority on this head. The court insisted that the authority of parliament went no farther than to remonstrate or show reasons against the tax, reserving to itself the right of determining whether the reasons were well- or ill-founded; and in consequence thereof, either to withdraw the edict as a matter of choice, or to order it to be registered as a matter of authority. The parliaments on their part insisted that they had not only a right to remonstrate, but to reject; and on this ground they were always supported by the nation.

But to return to the order of my narrative. M. Calonne wanted money; and as he knew the sturdy disposition of the parliaments with respect to new taxes, he ingeniously sought either to approach them by a more gentle means than that of direct authority, or to get over their heads by a manœuvre: and for this purpose he revived the project of assembling a body of men from the several provinces, under the style of an "assembly of the notables," or men of note, who met in 1787, and were either to recommend taxes to the parliaments or to act as a parliament themselves. An assembly under this name had been called in 1687.

As we are to view this as the first practical step towards the revolution, it will be proper to enter into some particulars respecting it. The assembly of the notables has in some places been mistaken for the states-general, but was wholly a different body; the states-general being always by election. The persons who composed the assembly of the notables were all nominated by the king, and consisted of one hundred and forty members. But as M. Calonne could not depend upon a majority of this assembly in his favor, he very ingeniously arranged them in such a manner as to make forty-four a majority of one hundred and forty: to effect this, he disposed of them into seven separate committees, of twenty members each. Every general question was to be decided, not by a majority of persons, but by a majority of committees; and as eleven votes would make a majority in a committee, and four committees a majority of seven, M. Calonne had good reason to conclude, that as forty-four would determine any general question, he could not be outvoted. But all his plans deceived him, and in the event became his overthrow.

The then Marquis de la Fayette was placed in the second committee, of which Count d'Artois was president; and as money matters was the object, it naturally brought into view every circumstance connected with it. M. de la Fayette made a verbal charge against Calonne for selling crown land to the amount of two millions of livres, in a manner that appeared to be unknown to the king. The Count d'Artois (as if to intimidate, for the Bastile was then in being) asked the marquis if he would render the charge in writing. He replied that he would. The Count d'Artois did not demand it, but brought a message from the king to that purport. M. de la Fayette then delivered in his charge in writing to be given to the king, undertaking to support it. No further proceedings were had upon this affair; but M. Calonne was soon after dismissed by the king, and went to England.

As M. de la Fayette, from the experience he had had in America, was better acquainted with the science of civil government than the generality of the members who composed the assembly of the notables could then be, the brunt of the business fell considerably to his share. The plan of those who had a constitution in view was to contend with the court on the ground of taxes, and some of them openly professed their object. Disputes frequently arose between Count d'Artois and M. de la Fayette upon various subjects. With respect to the arrears already incurred, the latter proposed to remedy them by accommodating the expenses to the revenue, instead of the revenue to the expenses; and as objects of reform, he proposed to abolish the Bastile and all the state prisons throughout the nation (the keeping of which was attended with great expense), and to suppress *lettres de cachet;* but those matters were not then much attended to; and with respect to *lettres de cachet, a majority of the nobles appeared to be in favor of them.*

On the subject of supplying the treasury by new taxes, the assembly declined taking the matter on themselves, concurring in the opinion that they had not authority. In a debate on the subject, M. de la Fayette said that raising money by taxes could only be done by a national assembly, freely elected by the people and acting as their representatives. Do you mean, said the Count d'Artois, the states-general? M. de la Fayette replied that he did. Will you, said the Count d'Artois, sign what you say, to be given to the king? The other replied that he not only would do this, but that he would go further, and say that the effectual mode would be for the king to agree to the establishment of a constitution.

As one of the plans had thus failed, that of getting the assembly to act as a parliament, the other came into view, that of recommending. On this subject the assembly agreed to recommend two new taxes to be enregistered by the parliament, the one a stamp act, and the other a territorial tax, or sort of land tax. The two have been estimated at about five millions sterling per annum. We have now to turn our attention to the parliaments, on whom the business was again devolving.

The archbishop of Toulouse (since archbishop of Sens, and now a cardinal) was appointed to the administration of the finances soon after the dismission of Calonne. He was also made prime minister, an office that did not always exist in France. When this office did not exist the chief of each of the principal departments transacted business immediately with the king; but when a prime minister was appointed, they did business only with him. The archbishop arrived to more state-authority than any minister since the Duke de Choiseuil, and the nation was strongly disposed in his favor; but by a line of conduct scarcely to be accounted for, he perverted every opportunity, turned out a despot, and sunk into disgrace, and a cardinal.

The assembly of the notables having broke up, the new minister sent the edicts for the two new taxes recommended by the assembly to the parliaments, to be enregistered. They of course came first before the parliament of Paris, who returned for answer, *That with such a revenue as the nation then supported, the name of taxes ought not to be mentioned but for the purpose of reducing them;* and threw both the edicts out.[1]

On this refusal, the parliament was ordered to Versailles, where in the usual form the king held what under the old government was called a bed of justice; and the two edicts were enregistered in presence of the parliament, by an order of state, in the manner mentioned. On this, the parliament immediately returned to Paris, renewed their session in form, and ordered the enregistering to be struck out, declaring that everything done at Versailles was illegal. All the members of parliament were then served with *lettres de cachet*, and exiled to Trois; but as they continued as inflexible in exile as before, and as vengeance did not supply the place of taxes, they were after a short time recalled to Paris.

The edicts were again tendered to them, and the Count d'Artois undertook to act as representative for the king. For this purpose he came from Versailles to Paris, in a train of procession; and the parliament was assembled to receive him. But show and parade had lost their influence in France; and whatever ideas of importance he might set off with, he had to return with those of mortification and disappointment. On alighting from his carriage to ascend the steps of the parliament house, the crowd (which was numerously collected) threw out trite expressions, saying, "This is Monsieur d'Artois, who wants more of our money to spend." The marked disapprobation which he saw impressed him with apprehensions; and the word

[1]When the English minister, Mr. Pitt, mentions the French finances again in the English parliament, it would be well that he noticed this as an example.

aux armes (*to arms*) was given out by the officer of the guard who attended him. It was so loudly vociferated that it echoed through the avenues of the house, and produced a temporary confusion: I was then standing in one of the apartments through which he had to pass, and could not avoid reflecting how wretched is the condition of a disrespected man.

He endeavored to impress the parliament by great words, and opened his authority by saying, "The king, our lord and master." The parliament received him very coolly and with their usual determination not to register the taxes; and in this manner the interview ended.

After this a new subject took place: in the various debates and contests that arose between the court and the parliaments on the subject of taxes, the parliament of Paris at last declared that although it had been customary for parliaments to enregister edicts for taxes as a matter of convenience, the right belonged only to the states-general; and that, therefore, the parliament could no longer with propriety continue to debate on what it had not authority to act. The king, after this, came to Paris and held a meeting with the parliament, in which he continued from ten in the morning till about six in the evening; and in a manner that appeared to proceed from him, as if unconsulted upon with the cabinet or the ministry, gave his word to the parliament that the states-general should be convened.

But after this another scene arose, on a ground different from all the former. The minister and the cabinet were averse to calling the states-general; they well knew, that if the states-general were assembled, that themselves must fall; and as the king had not mentioned *any time*, they hit on a project calculated to elude, without appearing to oppose.

For this purpose the court set about making a sort of constitution itself; it was principally the work of M. Lamoignon, keeper of the seals, who afterwards shot himself. The arrangement consisted in establishing a body under the name of a *cour plénière*, or full court, in which were invested all the power that the government might have occasion to make use of. The persons composing this court to be nominated by the king;

the contended right of taxation was given up on the part of the king, and a new criminal code of laws, and law proceedings, was substituted in the room of the former. The thing, in many points, contained better principles than those upon which the government had hitherto been administered; but, with respect to the *cour plénière*, it was no other than a medium through which despotism was to pass without appearing to act directly from itself.

The cabinet had high expectations from their new contrivance. The persons who were to compose the *cour plénière* were already nominated; and as it was necessary to carry a fair appearance, many of the best characters in the nation were appointed among the number. It was to commence on the 8th of May, 1788: but an opposition arose to it on two grounds—the one as to principle, the other as to form.

On the ground of principle, it was contended that government had not a right to alter itself; and that if the practice was once admitted, it would grow into a principle and be made a precedent for any future alterations the government might wish to establish; that the right of altering the government was a national right, and not a right of government. And on the ground of form, it was contended that the *cour plénière* was nothing more than a large cabinet.

The then Dukes de la Rochefoucault, Luxembourg, de Noailles, and many others, refused to accept the nomination, and strenuously opposed the whole plan. When the edict for establishing this new court was sent to the parliaments to be enregistered and put into execution, they resisted also. The parliament of Paris not only refused, but denied the authority; and the contest renewed itself between the parliament and the cabinet more strongly than ever. While the parliament was sitting in debate on this subject, the ministry ordered a regiment of soldiers to surround the house and form a blockade. The members sent out for beds and provision, and lived as in a besieged citadel; and as this had no effect, the commanding officer was ordered to enter the parliament house and seize them, which he did, and some of the principal members were shut up in different prisons. About the same time a deputation of persons arrived from the province of Brittany to remonstrate against the establishment of the *cour plénière*; and those the archbishop sent to the Bastile. But the spirit of the nation was not to be overcome; and it was so fully sensible of the strong ground it had taken, that of withholding taxes, that it contented itself with keeping up a sort of quiet resistance which effectually overthrew all the plans at that time formed against it. The project of the *cour plénière* was at last obliged to be given up, and the prime minister not long afterwards followed its fate; and M. Neckar was recalled into office.

The attempt to establish the *cour plénière* had an effect upon the nation which was not anticipated. It was a sort of new form of government that insensibly served to put the old one out of sight and to unhinge it from the superstitious authority of antiquity. It was government dethroning government; and the old one, by attempting to make a new one, made a chasm.

The failure of this scheme renewed the subject of convening the states-general: and this gave rise to a new series of politics. There was no settled form for convening the states-general; all that it positively meant was a deputation from what was then called the clergy, the nobility, and the commons; but their numbers, or their proportions, had not been always the same. They had been convened only on extraordinary occasions, the last of which was in 1614; their numbers were then in equal proportions, and they voted by orders.

It could not well escape the sagacity of M. Neckar that the mode of 1614 would answer neither the purpose of the then government, nor of the nation. As matters were at that time circumstanced, it would have been too contentious to argue upon anything. The debates would have been endless upon privileges and exemptions, in which neither the wants of the government nor the wishes of the nation for a constitution would have been attended to. But as he did not choose to take the decision upon himself, he summoned again the assembly of the *notables*, and referred it to them. This body was in general interested in the decision, being chiefly of the aristocracy and the high paid clergy; and they decided in favor of the mode of 1614. This decision was against the sense of the nation and also against the wishes of the court; for the aristocracy opposed itself to both and contended for privileges independent of either. The subject was then taken up by the parliament, who recommended that the number of the commons should be equal to the other two; and that they should all sit in one house, and vote in one body. The number finally determined on was twelve hundred: six hundred to be chosen by the commons (and this was less than their proportion ought to have been when their worth and consequence is considered on a national scale), three hundred by the clergy, and three hundred by the aristocracy; but with respect to the mode of assembling themselves, whether together or apart, or the manner in which they should vote, those matters were referred.[1]

[1] Mr. Burke (and I must take the liberty of telling him that he is unacquainted with French affairs), speaking upon this subject, says, "The first thing that struck me in calling the states-general, was a great departure from the ancient course;" and he soon after says, "From the moment I read the list, I saw distinctly, and very nearly as it has happened, all that was to follow." Mr. Burke certainly did not see all that was to follow. I have endeavored to impress him, as well before as after the states-general met, that there would be a *revolution;* but was not able to make him see it, neither would he believe it. How then he could distinctly see all the parts, when the whole was out of sight, is beyond my comprehension. And with respect to the "departure from the ancient course," besides the natural weakness of the remark, it shows that he is unacquainted with circumstances. The departure was necessary, from the experience had upon it, that the ancient course was a bad one. The states-general of 1614 were called at the commencement of the civil war in the minority of Louis XIII; but by the clash of arranging them by orders, they increased the confusion they were called to compose. The author of *l'Intrigue du Cabinet* (Vol. I, p. 329), who wrote before any revolution was thought of in France, speaking of the states-general of 1614, says, "They held the public in suspense five months; and by the questions agitated therein, and the heat with which they were put, it appears that the great (*les grands*) thought more to satisfy their particular passions than to procure the good of the nation; and the whole time passed away in altercations, ceremonies and parade."

The election that followed was not a contested election, but an animated one. The candidates were not men, but principles. Societies were formed in Paris, and committees of correspondence and communication established throughout the nation, for the purpose of enlightening the people and explaining to them the principles of civil government; and so orderly was the election conducted that it did not give rise even to the rumor of tumult.

The states-general were to meet at Versailles in April, 1789, but did not assemble till May. They located themselves in three separate chambers, or rather the clergy and the aristocracy withdrew each into a separate chamber. The majority of the aristocracy claimed what they call the privilege of voting as a separate body, and of giving their consent or their negative in that manner; and many of the bishops and high-beneficed clergy claimed the same privilege on the part of their order.

The *tiers état* (as they were called) disowned all knowledge of artificial orders and privileges; and they were not only resolute on this point but somewhat disdainful. They began to consider aristocracy as a kind of fungus growing out of the corruption of society, that could not be admitted even as a branch of it; and from the disposition the aristocracy had shown by upholding *lettres de cachet* and in sundry other instances, it was manifest that no constitution could be formed by admitting men in any other character than as national men.

After various altercations on this head, the *tiers état*, or commons (as they were then called), declared themselves (on a motion made for that purpose by the Abbé Sieyès) "THE REPRESENTATIVES OF THE NATION; *and that the two orders could be considered but as deputies of corporations, and could only have a deliberative voice but when they assembled in a national character, with the national representatives.*" This proceeding extinguished the style of *états généraux* or states-general, and erected it into the style it now bears, that of *l'assemble nationale* or national assembly.

This motion was not made in a precipitate manner: it was the result of cool deliberation, and concerted between the national representatives and the patriotic members of the two chambers, who saw into the folly, mischief, and injustice of artificial privileged distinctions. It was become evident that no constitution, worthy of being called by that name, could be established on anything less than a national ground. The aristocracy had hitherto opposed the despotism of the court and affected the language of patriotism; but it opposed it as its rival (as the English barons opposed King John); and it now opposed the nation from the same motives.

On carrying this motion the national representatives, as had been concerted, sent an invitation to the two chambers to unite with them in a national character, and proceed to business. A majority of the clergy, chiefly of the parish priests, withdrew from the clerical chamber and joined the nation; and forty-five from the other chamber joined in like manner. There is a sort of secret history belonging to this last circumstance which is necessary to its explanation; it was not judged prudent that all the patriotic members of the chamber, styling itself the nobles, should quit it at once; and in consequence of this arrangement, they drew off by degrees, always leaving some, as well to reason the case as to watch the suspected. In a little time the numbers increased from forty-five to eighty, and soon after to a greater number; which with a majority of the clergy, and the whole of the national representatives, put the malcontents in a very diminutive condition.

The king who, very different to the general class called by that name, is a man of a good heart, showed himself disposed to recommend a union of the three chambers on the ground the national assembly had taken; but the malcontents exerted themselves to prevent it, and began now to have another project in view. Their numbers consisted of a majority of the aristocratical chamber, and a minority of the clerical chamber, chiefly of bishops and high beneficed clergy; and these men were determined to put everything at issue, as well by strength as by stratagem. They had no objection to a constitution; but it must be such a one as themselves should dictate, and suited to their own views and particular situations. On the other hand the nation disowned knowing anything of them but as citizens, and was determined to shut out all such upstart pretensions. The more aristocracy appeared, the more it was despised; there was a visible imbecility and want of intellects in the majority, a sort of *je ne sais quoi*, that while it affected to be more than citizen, was less than man. It lost ground more from contempt than from hatred; and was rather jeered at as an ass, than dreaded as a lion. This is the general character of aristocracy, or what are called nobles or nobility, or rather no-ability, in all countries.

The plan of the malcontents consisted now of two things; either to deliberate and vote by chambers (or orders), more especially on all questions respecting a constitution (by which the aristocratical chamber would have had a negative on any article of the constitution), or in case they could not accomplish this object, to overthrow the national assembly entirely.

To effect one or the other of these objects, they began now to cultivate a friendship with the despotism they had hitherto attempted to rival, and the Count d'Artois became their chief. The king (who has since declared himself deceived into their measures) held, according to the old form, *a bed of justice*, in which he accorded to the deliberation and vote *par tête* (by head) upon several objects; but reserved the deliberation and vote upon all questions respecting a constitution to the three chambers separately. This declaration of the king was made against the advice of M. Neckar, who now began to perceive that he was growing out of fashion at court, and that another minister was in contemplation.

As the form of sitting in separate chambers was yet apparently kept up, though essentially destroyed, the national representatives, immediately after this declaration of the king, resorted to their chambers to consult on a protest against it; and the minority of the chamber (calling itself the nobles) who had joined the national cause retired to a private house to consult in like manner. The malcontents had by this time concerted their measures with the court, which Count d'Artois undertook to conduct; and as they saw from the discontent which the declaration excited, and the opposition making against it, that they could not obtain a control over the intended constitution by a separate vote, they prepared themselves for their final object— that of conspiring against the national assembly and overthrowing it.

The next morning the door of the chamber of the national assembly was shut against them, and guarded by troops; and the members were refused admittance. On this they withdrew to a tennis ground in the neighborhood of Versailles, as the most convenient place they could find, and after renewing their session, took an oath never to separate from each other, under any circumstances whatever, death excepted, until they had established a constitution. As the experiment of shutting up the house had no other effect than that of producing a closer connection in the members, it was opened again the next day, and the public business recommenced in the usual place.

We now are to have in view the forming the new ministry which was to accomplish the overthrow of the national assembly. But as force would be necessary, orders were issued to assemble thirty thousand troops, the command of which was given to Broglio, one of the new-intended ministry, who was recalled from the country for this purpose. But as some management was necessary to keep this plan concealed till the moment it should be ready for execution, it is to this policy that a declaration made by the Count d'Artois must be attributed, and which is here proper to be introduced.

It could not but occur, that while the malcontents continued to resort to their chambers separate from the national assembly, that more jealousy would be excited than if they were mixed with it, and that the plot might be suspected. But as they had taken their ground, and now wanted a pretense for quitting it, it was necessary that one should be devised. This was effectually accomplished by a declaration made by Count d'Artois, that *"if they took not a part in the national assembly, the life of the king would be endangered,"* on which they quitted their chambers and mixed with the assembly in one body.

At the time this declaration was made, it was generally treated as a piece of absurdity in the Count d'Artois, and calculated merely to relieve the outstanding members of the two chambers from the diminutive situation they were put in; and if nothing more had followed, this conclusion would have been good. But as things best explain themselves by events, this apparent union was only a cover to the machinations that were secretly going on, and the declaration accommodated itself to answer that purpose. In a little time the national assembly found itself surrounded by troops, and thousands daily arriving. On this a very strong declaration was made by the national assembly to the king, remonstrating on the impropriety of the measure, and demanding the reason. The king, who was not in the secret of this business, as himself afterwards declared, gave substantially for answer that he had no other object in view than to preserve public tranquillity, which appeared to be much disturbed.

But in a few days from this time the plot unravelled itself. M. Neckar and the ministry were displaced, and a new one formed of the enemies of the revolution; and Broglio, with between twenty-five and thirty thousand foreign troops, was arrived to support them. The mask was now thrown off, and matters were come to a crisis. The event was that in the space of three days the new ministry and all their abettors found it prudent to fly the nation; the Bastile was taken, and Broglio and his foreign troops dispersed; as is already related in a former part of this work.

There are some curious circumstances in the history of this short-lived ministry, and this brief attempt at a counter-revolution. The palace of Versailles, where the court was sitting, was not more than four hundred yards distant from the hall where the national assembly was sitting. The two places were at this moment like the separate headquarters of two combatant enemies; yet the court was as perfectly ignorant of the information which had arrived from Paris to the national assembly, as if it had resided at a hundred miles distance. The then Marquis de la Fayette, who (as has been already mentioned) was chosen to preside in the national assembly on this particular occasion, named, by order of the assembly, three successive deputations to the king, on the day and up to the evening on which the Bastile was taken, to inform and confer with him on the state of affairs; but the ministry, who knew not so much as that it was attacked, precluded all communication and were solacing themselves how dexterously they had succeeded: but in a few hours the accounts arrived so thick and fast, that they had to start from their desks and run; some set off in one disguise, and some in another, and none in their own character. Their anxiety now was to outride the news lest they should be stopped, which, though it flew fast, flew not so fast as themselves.

It is worth remarking that the national assembly neither pursued those fugitive conspirators, nor took any notice of them, nor sought to retaliate in any shape whatever. Occupied with establishing a constitution founded on the rights of man and the authority of the people, the only authority on which government has a right to exist in any country, the national assembly felt none of those mean passions which mark the character of impertinent governments, founding themselves on their own authority, or on the absurdity of hereditary succession. It is the faculty of the human mind to become what it contemplates, and to act in unison with its object.

[THE FRENCH DECLARATION OF RIGHTS]

One of the first works of the national assembly, instead of vindictive proclamations as has been the case with other governments, published a declaration of the rights of man as the basis on which the new constitution was to be built, and which is here subjoined:

Declaration of the Rights of Man and of Citizens

"The representatives of the people of France, formed into a national assembly, considering that ignorance, neglect, or contempt of human rights, are the sole causes of public misfortunes, and corruptions of government, have resolved to set forth, in a solemn declaration, these natural, imprescriptible, and unalienable rights: that this declaration being constantly present to the minds of the body social, they may be ever kept attentive to their rights and their duties: that the acts of the legislative and executive powers of government, being capable of being every moment compared with the end of political institutions, may be more respected: and also, that the future claims of the citizens, being directed by simple and incontestible principles, may always tend to the maintenance of the constitution and the general happiness.

"For these reasons the national assembly doth recognize and declare, in the presence of the supreme being, and with a hope of his blessing and favor, the following *sacred* rights of men and of citizens:

"I. Men are born and always continue free and equal in respect of their rights. Civil distinctions, therefore, can only be founded on public utility.

"II. The end of all political associations is the preservation of the natural and imprescriptible rights of man; and these rights are liberty, property, security, and resistance of oppression.

"III. The nation is essentially the source of all sovereignty: nor can any *individual* or *any body of men*, be entitled to any authority which is not expressly derived from it.

"IV. Political liberty consists in the power of doing whatever does not injure another. The exercise of the natural rights of every man has no other limits than those which are necessary to secure to every *other* man the free exercise of the same rights; and these limits are determinable only by the law.

"V. The law ought to prohibit only actions hurtful to society. What is not prohibited by the law, should not be hindered; nor should anyone be compelled to that which the law does not require.

"VI. The law is an expression of the will of the community. All citizens have a right to concur, either personally, or by their representatives, in its formation. It should be the same to all, whether it protects or punishes; and all being equal in its sight, are equally eligible to all honors, places, and employments, according to their different abilities, without any other distinction than that created by their virtues and talents.

"VII. No man should be accused, arrested, or held in confinement, except in cases determined by the law, and according to the forms which it has prescribed. All who promote, solicit, execute, or cause to be executed, arbitrary orders, ought to be punished; and every citizen called upon or apprehended by virtue of the law, ought immediately to obey, and not render himself culpable by resistance.

"VIII. The law ought to impose no other penalties than such as are absolutely and evidently necessary: and no one ought to be punished, but in virtue of a law promulgated before the offense, and legally applied.

"IX. Every man being presumed innocent till he has been convicted, whenever his detention becomes indispensable, all rigor to him, more than is necessary to secure his person, ought to be provided against by the law.

"X. No man ought to be molested on account of his opinions, not even on account of his religious opinions, provided his avowal of them does not disturb the public order established by law.

"XI. The unrestrained communication of thoughts and opinions being one of the most precious rights of man, every citizen may speak, write, and publish freely, provided he is responsible for the abuse of this liberty in cases determined by the law.

"XII. A public force being necessary to give security to the rights of men and of citizens, that force is instituted for the benefit of the community, and not for the particular benefit of the persons with whom it is entrusted.

"XIII. A common contribution being necessary for the support of the public force, and for defraying the other expenses of government, it ought to be divided equally among the members of the community, according to their abilities.

"XIV. Every citizen has a right, either by himself or his representative, to a free voice in determining the necessity of public contributions, the appropriation of them, and their amount, mode of assessment, and duration.

"XV. Every community has a right to demand of all its agents, an account of their conduct.

"XVI. Every community in which a separation of powers and a security of rights is not provided for, wants a constitution.

"XVII. The right to property being inviolable and sacred, no one ought to be deprived of it, except in cases of evident public necessity legally ascertained, and on condition of a previous just indemnity."

[OBSERVATIONS ON THE DECLARATION]

The three first articles comprehend in general terms the whole of a declaration of rights: all the succeeding articles either originate out of them, or follow as elucidations. The 4th, 5th, and 6th, define more particularly what is only generally expressed in the 1st, 2d, and 3d.

The 7th, 8th, 9th, 10th, and 11th articles are declaratory of *principles* upon which laws shall be construed conformable to *rights* already declared. But it is questioned by some very good people in France, as well as in other countries, whether the 10th article sufficiently guarantees the right it is intended to accord with; besides which, it takes off from the divine dignity of religion, and weakens its operative force upon the mind to make it a subject of human laws. It then presents itself to man, like light intercepted by a cloudy medium, in which the source of it is obscured from his sight, and he sees nothing to reverence in the dusky rays.[1]

The remaining articles, beginning with the twelfth, are substantially contained in the principles of the preceding articles; but, in the particular situation in which France then was, having to undo what was wrong, as well as to set up what was right, it

[1] There is a single idea which, if it strikes rightly upon the mind, either in a legal or a religious sense, will prevent any man, or any body of men, or any government, from going wrong on the subject of religion: which is, that before any human institutions of government were known in the world, there existed, if I may so express it, a compact between God and man from the beginning of time; and that as the relation and condition which man in his individual person stands in towards his maker cannot be changed by any human laws or human authority, that religious devotion, which is a part of this compact, cannot so much as be made a subject of human laws; and that all laws must conform themselves to this prior existing compact, and not assume to make the compact conform to the laws which, besides being human, are subsequent thereto. The first act of man, when he looked around and saw himself a creature which he did not make and a world furnished for his reception, must have been devotion; and devotion must ever continue sacred to every individual man as it appears right to him; and governments do mischief by interfering.

was proper to be more particular than in another condition of things would be necessary.

While the declaration of rights was before the national assembly, some of its members remarked that if a declaration of rights was published it should be accompanied by a declaration of duties. The observation discovered a mind that reflected, and it only erred by not reflecting far enough. A declaration of rights is, by reciprocity, a declaration of duties also. Whatever is my right as a man, is also the right of another; and it becomes my duty to guarantee, as well as to possess.

The three first articles are the basis of liberty as well individual as national; nor can any country be called free whose government does not take its beginning from the principles they contain and continue to preserve them pure; and the whole of the declaration of rights is of more value to the world, and will do more good, than all the laws and statutes that have yet been promulgated.

In the declaratory exordium which prefaces the declaration of rights, we see the solemn and majestic spectacle of a nation opening its commission, under the auspices of its Creator, to establish a government; a scene so new, and so transcendently unequalled by anything in the European world, that the name of a revolution is inexpressive of its character, and it rises into a regeneration of man. What are the present governments of Europe but a scene of iniquity and oppression? What is that of England? Do not its own inhabitants say it is a market where every man has his price, and where corruption is common traffic, at the expense of a deluded people? No wonder, then, that the French revolution is traduced. Had it confined itself merely to the destruction of flagrant despotism, perhaps Mr. Burke and some others had been silent. Their cry now is, "It has gone too far": that is, gone too far for them. It stares corruption in the face, and the venal tribe are all alarmed. Their fear discovers itself in their outrage, and they are but publishing the groans of a wounded vice. But from such opposition, the French revolution, instead of suffering, receives homage. The more it is struck, the more sparks it will emit; and the fear is, it will not be struck enough. It has nothing to dread from attacks. Truth has given it an establishment; and time will record it with a name as lasting as its own.

MISCELLANEOUS CHAPTER

To prevent interrupting the argument in the preceding part of this work, or the narrative that follows it, I reserved some observations to be thrown together into a miscellaneous chapter; by which variety might not be censured for confusion. Mr. Burke's book is *all* miscellany. His intention was to make an attack on the French revolution; but instead of proceeding with an orderly arrangement, he has stormed it with a mob of ideas, tumbling over and destroying one another.

But this confusion and contradiction in Mr. Burke's book is easily accounted for. When a man in any cause attempts to steer his course by anything else than some popular truth or principle, he is sure to be lost. It is beyond the compass of his capacity to keep all the parts of an argument together, and make them unite in one issue, by any other means than having his guide always in view. Neither memory nor invention will supply the want of it. The former fails him, and the latter betrays him.

Notwithstanding the nonsense, for it deserves no better name, that Mr. Burke has asserted about hereditary rights, and hereditary succession, and that a nation has not a right to form a government for itself, it happened to fall in his way to give some account of what government is. "Government," says he, "is a contrivance of human wisdom."

Admitting that government is a contrivance of human wisdom, it must necessarily follow that hereditary succession and hereditary rights (as they are called) can make no part of it, because it is impossible to make wisdom hereditary; and, on the other hand, *that* cannot be a wise contrivance which in its operation may commit the government of a nation to the wisdom of an idiot. The ground which Mr. Burke now takes is fatal to every part of his cause. The argument changes from hereditary rights to hereditary wisdom; and the question is, who is the wisest man? He must now show that everyone in the line of hereditary succession was a Solomon, or his title is not good to be a king. What a stroke has Mr. Burke now made! To use a sailor's phrase he has *swabbed the deck*, and scarcely left a name legible in the list of kings; and he has mowed down and thinned the house of peers with a scythe as formidable as death and time.

But Mr. Burke appears to have been aware of this retort, and he has taken care to guard against it by making government to be not only a *contrivance* of human wisdom, but a *monopoly* of wisdom. He puts the nation as fools on one side, and places his government of wisdom, all wise men of Gotham, on the other side; and he then proclaims and says that "*men have a* RIGHT *that their* WANTS *should be provided for by this wisdom.*" Having thus made proclamation, he next proceeds to explain to them what their *wants* are, and also what their *rights* are. In this he has succeeded dexterously, for he makes their wants to be a *want* of wisdom; but as this is but cold comfort, he then informs them that they have a *right* (not to any of the wisdom) but to be governed by it; and in order to impress them with a solemn reverence for this monopoly-government of wisdom, and of its vast capacity for all purposes, possible or impossible, right or wrong, he proceeds with astrological, mysterious importance, to tell them its powers in these words—"The rights of men in government are their advantages; and these are often in balances between differences of good; and in compromises sometimes between *good* and *evil*, and sometimes between *evil* and *evil*. Political reason is a *computing principle;* adding, subtracting, multiplying, and dividing, morally and not metaphysically or mathematically, true moral demonstrations."

As the wondering audience whom Mr. Burke supposes himself talking to may not understand all this jargon, I will undertake to be its interpreter. The meaning then, good people, of all this is *that government is governed by no principle whatever; that it can make evil good, or good evil, just as it pleases. In short, that government is arbitrary power.*

But there are some things which Mr. Burke has forgotten:

1st, he has not shown where the wisdom originally came from; and, 2d, he has not shown by what authority it first began to act. In the manner he introduced the matters, it is either government stealing wisdom, or wisdom stealing government. It is without an origin, and its powers without authority. In short, it is usurpation.

Whether it be from a sense of shame, or from a consciousness of some radical defect in government necessary to be kept out of sight, or from both, or from some other cause, I undertake not to determine; but so it is, that a monarchical reasoner never traces government to its source, or from its source. It is one of the *shibboleths* by which he may be known. A thousand years hence, those who shall live in America, or in France, will look back with contemplative pride on the origin of their governments, and say, *this was the work of our glorious ancestors!* But what can a monarchical talker say? What has he to exult in? Alas! he has nothing. A certain something forbids him to look back to a beginning, lest some robber, or some Robin Hood, should rise from the long obscurity of time and say, *I am the origin.* Hard as Mr. Burke labored under the regency bill and hereditary succession two years ago, and much as he dived for precedents, he still had not boldness enough to bring up William of Normandy and say, *there is the head of the list, there is the fountain of honor,* the son of a prostitute, and the plunderer of the English nation.

The opinions of men, with respect to government, are changing fast in all countries. The revolutions of America and France have thrown a beam of light over the world, which reaches into man. The enormous expense of governments has provoked people to think by making them feel; and when once the veil begins to rend, it admits not of repair. Ignorance is of a peculiar nature; once dispelled, it is impossible to re-establish it. It is not originally a thing of itself, but is only the absence of knowledge; and though man may be *kept* ignorant, he cannot be *made* ignorant. The mind in discovering truths acts in the same manner as it acts through the eye in discovering an object; when once any object has been seen, it is impossible to put the mind back to the same condition it was in before it saw it. Those who talk of a counter-revolution in France show how little they understand of man. There does not exist in the compass of language an arrangement of words to express so much as the means of effecting a counter-revolution. The means must be an obliteration of knowledge; and it has never yet been discovered how to make a man *unknow* his knowledge, or *unthink* his thoughts.

Mr. Burke is laboring in vain to stop the progress of knowledge; and it comes with the worse grace from him, as there is a certain transaction known in the city, which renders him suspected of being a pensioner in a fictitious name. This may account for some strange doctrine he has advanced in his book, which, though he points it at the Revolution society, is effectually directed against the whole nation.

"The king of England," says he, "holds *his* crown (for it does not belong to the nation, according to Mr. Burke) in *contempt* of the choice of the Revolution society, who have not a single vote for a king among them either *individually* or *collectively;* and his majesty's heirs, each in his time and order, will come to the crown *with the same contempt* of their choice with which his majesty has succeeded to that which he now wears."

As to who is king of England or elsewhere, or whether there is any at all, or whether the people choose a Cherokee chief, or a Hessian hussar for a king, is not a matter that I trouble myself about, be that to themselves; but with respect to the doctrine, so far as it relates to the rights of men and nations, it is as abominable as anything ever uttered in the most enslaved country under heaven. Whether it sounds worse to my ear, by not being accustomed to hear such despotism, than it does to the ear of another person, I am not so well a judge of; but of its abominable principle, I am at no loss to judge.

It is not the Revolution society that Mr. Burke means; it is the nation, as well in its *original* as in its *representative* character; and he has taken care to make himself understood, by saying that they have not a vote either *collectively* or *individually*. The Revolution society is composed of citizens of all denominations, and of members of both houses of parliament, and consequently, if there is not a right to vote in any of the characters, there can be no right to any, either in the nation or in its parliament. This ought to be a caution to every country, how it imports foreign families to be kings. It is somewhat curious to observe that although the people of England have been in the habit of talking about the kings, it is always a foreign house of kings; hating foreigners, yet governed by them. It is now the house of Brunswick, one of the petty tribes of Germany.

It has hitherto been the practice of the English parliaments to regulate what was called the succession (taking it for granted that the nation then continued to accord to the form of annexing a monarchical branch to its government; for without this, the parliament could not have had authority to have sent either to Holland or to Hanover, or to impose a king upon a nation against its will). And this must be the utmost limit to which parliament can go upon the case; but the right of the nation goes to the *whole* case, because it is the right of changing the *whole* form of government. The right of a parliament is only a right in trust, a right by delegation, and that but from a very small part of the nation; and one of its houses has not even this. But the right of the nation is an original right, as universal as taxation. The nation is the paymaster of everything, and everything must conform to its general will.

I remember taking notice of a speech in what is called the English house of peers by the then Earl of Shelbourne, and I think it was at the time he was minister, which is applicable to this case. I do not directly charge my memory with every particular; but the words and the purport as nearly as I remember were these, *that the form of government was a matter wholly at the will of a nation at all times; that if it chose a monarchical form, it had a right to have it so, and if it afterwards chose to be a republic, it had a right to be a republic, and to say to a king, we have no longer any occasion for you.*

When Mr. Burke says that "his majesty's heirs and successors, each in their time and order, will come to the crown with the same contempt of their choice with which his majesty has succeeded to that he wears," it is saying too much even to the humblest individual in the country, part of whose daily labor goes towards making up the million sterling a year which the country gives a person it styles a king. Government with insolence is despotism; but when contempt is added, it becomes worse; and to pay for contempt is the excess of slavery. This species of government comes from Germany; and reminds me of what one of the Brunswick soldiers told me, who was taken prisoner by the Americans in the late war; "Ah!" said he, "America is a fine free country, it is worth people's fighting for; I know the difference by knowing my own; in my country, if the prince say, eat straw, we eat straw." God help that country, thought I, be it England or elsewhere, whose liberties are not to be protected by German principles of government and princes of Brunswick.

As Mr. Burke sometimes speaks of England, sometimes of France, and sometimes of the world and of government in general, it is difficult to answer his book without apparently meeting him on the same ground. Although principles of government are general subjects, it is next to impossible in many cases to separate them from the idea of place and circumstance; and the more so when circumstances are put for arguments, which is frequently the case with Mr. Burke.

In the former part of his book, addressing himself to the people of France, he says, "no experience has taught us (meaning the English) that in any other course or method than that of an *hereditary crown*, can our liberties be regularly perpetuated and preserved sacred as our *hereditary right*." I ask Mr. Burke who is to take them away? M. de la Fayette, in speaking of France, says, "*For a nation to be free, it is sufficient that she wills it*." But Mr. Burke represents England as wanting capacity to take care of itself; and that its liberties must be taken care of by a king holding it in "contempt." If England is sunk to this, it is preparing itself to eat straw, as in Hanover or in Brunswick. But besides the folly of the declaration, it happens that the facts are all against Mr. Burke. It was by the government *being hereditary* that the liberties of the people were endangered.

Charles I and James II are instances of this truth, yet neither of them went so far as to hold the nation in contempt.

As it is sometimes of advantage to the people of one country to hear what those of other countries have to say respecting it, it is possible that the people of France may learn something from Mr. Burke's book, and that the people of England may also learn something from the answers it will occasion. When nations fall out about freedom, a wide field of debate is opened. The argument commences with the rights of war, without its evils; and as knowledge is the object contended for, the party that sustains the defeat obtains the prize.

Mr. Burke talks about what he calls an hereditary crown, as if it were some production of nature; or as if, like time, it had power to operate not only independently but in spite of man; or as if it were a thing or a subject universally consented to. Alas! it has none of those properties, but is the reverse of them all. It is a thing of imagination, the propriety of which is more than doubted, and the legality of which in a few years will be denied.

But to arrange this matter in a clearer view than what general expressions can convey, it will be necessary to state the distinct heads under which (what is called) an hereditary crown, or, more properly speaking, an hereditary succession to the government of a nation, can be considered, which are,

1st, The right of a particular family to establish itself.

2d. The right of a nation to establish a particular family.

With respect to the *first* of these heads, that of a family establishing itself with hereditary powers on its own authority, and independent of the consent of a nation, all men will concur in calling it despotism; and it would be trespassing on their understanding to attempt to prove it.

But the *second* head, that of a nation establishing a particular family with *hereditary powers*, does not present itself as despotism on the first reflection; but if men will permit a second reflection to take place, and carry that reflection forward but one remove out of their own persons to that of their offspring, they will then see that hereditary succession becomes in its consequences the same despotism to others, which they reprobated for themselves. It operates to preclude the consent of the succeeding generation, and the preclusion of consent is despotism. When the person who at any time shall be in possession of a government, or those who stand in succession to him, shall say to a nation, I hold this power in "contempt" of you, it signifies not on what authority he pretends to say it. It is no relief, but an aggravation to a person in slavery, to reflect that he was sold by his parent; and as that which heightens the criminality of an act cannot be produced to prove the legality of it, hereditary succession cannot be established as a legal thing.

In order to arrive at a more perfect decision on this head, it will be proper to consider the generation which undertakes to establish a family with *hereditary powers* separately from the generations which are to follow; and also to consider the character in which the *first* generation acts with respect to succeeding generations.

The generation which selects a person and puts him at the head of its government, either with the title of king or any other distinction, acts its *own choice*, be it wise or foolish, as a free agent for itself. The person so set up is not hereditary, but selected and appointed; and the generation who sets him up does not live under an hereditary government, but under a government of its own choice and establishment. Were the generation who sets him up, and the person so set up, to live forever, it never could become hereditary succession; hereditary succession can only follow on death of the first parties.

As therefore hereditary succession is out of the question with respect to the *first* generation, we have now to consider the character in which *that* generation acts with respect to the commencing generation and to all succeeding ones.

It assumes a character to which it has neither right nor title. It changes itself from a *legislator* to a *testator*, and affects to make its will, which is to have operation after the demise of the makers, to bequeath the government; and it not only attempts to bequeath, but to establish on the succeeding generation a new and different form of government under which itself lived. Itself, as is before observed, lived not under an hereditary government, but under a government of its own choice and establishment; and it now attempts by virtue of a will and testament (and which it has not authority to make) to take from the commencing generation and all future ones, the rights and free agency by which itself acted.

But exclusive of the right which any generation has to act collectively as a testator, the objects to which it applies itself in this case are not within the compass of any law, or of any will or testament.

The rights of men in society are neither devisable nor transferable nor annihilable, but are descendable only; and it is not in the power of any generation to intercept finally and cut off the descent. If the present generation, or any other, are disposed to be slaves, it does not lessen the right of the succeeding generation to be free: wrongs cannot have a legal descent. When Mr. Burke attempts to maintain that the *English nation did, at the revolution of 1688, most solemnly renounce and abdicate their rights for themselves, and for all their posterity forever*, he speaks a language that merits not reply, and which can only excite contempt for his prostitute principles, or pity for his ignorance.

In whatever light hereditary succession, as growing out of the will and testament of some former generation, presents itself, it is an absurdity. A cannot make a will to take from B his property, and give it to C; yet this is the manner in which (what is called) hereditary succession by law operates. A certain former generation made a will to take away the rights of the commencing generation and all future ones, and convey those rights to a third person, who afterwards comes forward and tells them, in Mr. Burke's language, that they have *no rights*, that their rights are already bequeathed to him, and that he will govern in *contempt* of them. From such principles, and such ignorance, good Lord deliver the world!

But, after all, what is this metaphor, called a crown, or rather, what is monarchy? Is it a thing, or is it a name, or is it a fraud? Is it a "contrivance of human wisdom," or human craft, to obtain money from a nation under specious pretenses? Is it a thing necessary to a nation? If it is, in what does that necessity consist, what service does it perform, what is its business, and what are its merits? Doth the virtue consist in the metaphor, or in the man? Doth the goldsmith that makes the crown, make the virtue also? Doth it operate like Fortunatus's wishing cap, or Harlequin's wooden sword? Doth it make a man a conjuror? In fine, what is it? It appears to be a something going much out of fashion, falling into ridicule, and rejected in some countries both as unnecessary and expensive. In America it is considered as an absurdity, and in France it has so far declined that the goodness of the man and the respect for his personal character are the only things that preserve the appearance of its existence.

If government be what Mr. Burke describes it, "a contrivance of human wisdom," I might ask him if wisdom was at such a low ebb in England that it was become necessary to import it from Holland and from Hanover? But I will do the country the justice to say that that was not the case; and even if it was, it mistook the cargo. The wisdom of every country, when properly exerted, is sufficient for all its purposes; and there could exist no more real occasion in England to have sent for a Dutch stadtholder, or a German elector, than there was in America to have done a similar thing. If a country does not understand its own affairs, how is a foreigner to understand them, who knows neither its laws, its manners, nor its language? If there existed a man so transcendently wise above all others that his wisdom was necessary to instruct a nation, some reason might be offered for monarchy; but when we cast our eyes about a country, and observe how every part understands its own affairs; and when we look around the world, and see that of all men in it, the race of kings are the most insignificant in capacity, our reason cannot fail to ask us, What are those men kept for?

If there is anything in monarchy which we people of America do not understand, I wish Mr. Burke would be so kind as to inform us. I see in America a government extending over a country ten times as large as England, and conducted with regularity for a fortieth part of the expense which government costs in England. If I ask a man in America if he wants a king, he retorts, and asks me if I take him for an idiot. How is it that this difference happens: are we more or less wise than others? I see in America the generality of the people living in a style of plenty unknown in monarchical countries; and I see that the principle of its government, which is that of the *equal rights of man*, is making a rapid progress in the world.

If monarchy is a useless thing, why is it kept up anywhere? And if a necessary thing, how can it be dispensed with? That *civil government* is necessary, all civilized nations will agree in; but civil government is republican government. All that part of the government of England which begins with the office of constable, and proceeds through the department of magistrate, quarter-session, and general assize, including the trial by jury, is republican government. Nothing of monarchy appears in any part of it, except the name which William the Conqueror imposed upon the English, that of obliging them to call him "their sovereign lord the king."

It is easy to conceive that a band of interested men, such as placemen, pensioners, lords of the bed-chamber, lords of the kitchen, lords of the necessary-house, and the Lord knows what besides, can find as many reasons for monarchy as their salaries, paid at the expense of the country, amount to; but if I ask the farmer, the manufacturer, the merchant, the trades-man, and down through all the occupations of life to the common laborer, what service monarchy is to him, he can give me no answer. If I ask him what monarchy is, he believes it is something like a sinecure.

Notwithstanding the taxes of England amount to almost seventeen million a year, said to be for the expenses of government, it is still evident that the sense of the nation is left to govern itself, and does govern itself by magistrates and juries, almost at its own charge, on republican principles, exclusive of the expense of taxes. The salaries of the judges are almost the only charge that is paid out of the revenue. Considering that all the internal government is executed by the people, the taxes of England ought to be the lightest of any nation in Europe; instead of which, they are the contrary. As this cannot be accounted for on the score of civil government, the subject necessarily extends itself to the monarchical part.

When the people of England sent for George I (and it would puzzle a wiser man than Mr. Burke to discover for what he could be wanted, or what service he could render) they ought at least to have conditioned for the abandonment of Hanover. Besides the endless German intrigues that must follow from a German elector's being king of England, there is a natural impossibility of uniting in the same person the principles of freedom and the principles of despotism, or, as it is called in England, arbitrary power. A German elector is, in his electorate, a despot: how then should it be expected that he should be attached to principles of liberty in one country, while his interest in another was to be supported by despotism? The union cannot exist; and it might easily have been foreseen that German electors would make German kings, or in Mr. Burke's words, would assume government with "contempt." The English have been in the habit of considering a king of England only in the character in which he appears to them; whereas the same person, while the connection lasts, has a home-seat in another country, the interest of which is at variance with their own, and the principles of the government in opposition to each other. To such a person England will appear as a town-residence, and the electorate as the estate. The English may wish, as I believe they do, success to the principles of liberty in France, or in Germany; but a German elector trembles for the fate of despotism in his electorate; and the duchy of Mecklenburg, where the present queen's family governs, is under the same wretched state of arbitrary power, and the people in slavish vassalage.

There never was a time when it became the English to watch continental intrigues more circumspectly than at the present moment, and to distinguish the politics of the electorate from the politics of the nation. The revolution of France has entirely changed the ground with respect to England and France, as nations; but the German despots, with Prussia at their head, are combining against liberty; and the fondness of Mr. Pitt for office, and the interest which all his family connections have obtained, do not give sufficient security against this intrigue.

As everything which passes in the world becomes matter for history, I will now quit this subject, and take a concise review of the state of parties and politics in England, as Mr. Burke has done in France.

Whether the present reign commenced with contempt, I leave to Mr. Burke: certain however it is that it had strongly that appearance. The animosity of the English nation, it is very well remembered, ran high: and had the true principles of liberty been as well understood then as they now promise to be, it is probable the nation would not have patiently submitted to so much. George I and II were sensible of a rival in the remains of the Stuarts; and as they could not but consider themselves as standing on their good behavior, they had prudence to keep their German principles of government to themselves; but as the Stuart family wore away, the prudence became less necessary.

The contest between rights and what were called prerogatives continued to heat the nation till some time after the conclusion of the American revolution, when all at once it fell a calm; execration exchanged itself for applause, and court popularity sprung up like a mushroom in the night.

To account for this sudden transition it is proper to observe that there are two distinct species of popularity; the one excited by merit, the other by resentment. As the nation had formed itself into two parties, and each was extolling the merits of its parliamentary champions for and against the prerogative, nothing could operate to give a more general shock than an immediate coalition of the champions themselves. The partisans of each being thus suddenly left in the lurch, and mutually heated with disgust at the measure, felt no other relief than uniting in a common execration against both. A higher stimu-

lus of resentment being thus excited than what the contest on
prerogatives had occasioned, the nation quitted all former
objects of rights and wrongs, and sought only that of gratifica-
tion. The indignation at the coalition so effectually superseded
the indignation against the court as to extinguish it, and without any change of principles on the part of the court, the same
people who had reprobated its despotism, united with it to
revenge themselves on the coalition parliament. The case was
not which they liked best—but which they hated most; and
the least hated passed for love. The dissolution of the coalition
parliament, as it afforded the means of gratifying the resentment of the nation, could not fail to be popular; and from
hence arose the popularity of the court.

Transitions of this kind exhibit to us a nation under the government of temper instead of a fixed and steady principle; and
having once committed itself, however rashly, it feels itself
urged along to justify by continuance its first proceeding.
Measures which at other times it would censure, it now ap-
proves, and acts persuasion upon itself to suffocate its judgment.

On the return of a new parliament, the new minister, Mr. Pitt,
found himself in a secure majority; and the nation gave him
credit, not out of regard to himself, but because it had resolved
to do it out of resentment to another. He introduced himself
to public notice by a proposed reform of parliament, which in
its operation would have amounted to a public justification of
corruption. The nation was to be at the expense of buying up
the rotten boroughs, whereas it ought to punish the persons
who deal in the traffic.

Passing over the two bubbles, of the Dutch business and the
million a year to sink the national debt, the matter which is
most prominent is the affair of the regency. Never in the
course of my observation was delusion more successfully acted,
nor a nation more completely deceived. But, to make this
appear, it will be necessary to go over the circumstances.

Mr. Fox had stated in the house of commons that the prince
of Wales, as heir in succession, had a right in himself to assume
the government. This was opposed by Mr. Pitt; and, so far

as the opposition was confined to the doctrine, it was just. But the principles which Mr. Pitt maintained on the contrary side were as bad or worse in their extent than those of Mr. Fox; because they went to establish an aristocracy over the nation, and over the small representation it has in the house of commons.

Whether the English form of government be good or bad, is not in this case the question; but, taking it as it stands, without regard to its merits or demerits, Mr. Pitt was further from the point than Mr. Fox.

It is supposed to consist of three parts; while, therefore, the nation is disposed to continue this form, the parts have a *national standing*, independent of each other, and are not the creatures of each other. Had Mr. Fox passed through parliament, and said that the person alluded to claimed on the ground of the nation, Mr. Pitt must then have contended for the right of the parliament, against the right of the nation.

By the appearance which the contest made, Mr. Fox took the hereditary ground; and Mr. Pitt the parliamentary ground, but the fact is they both took hereditary ground, and Mr. Pitt took the worse of the two.

What is called the parliament is made up of two houses; one of which is more hereditary and more beyond the control of the nation than what the crown (as it is called) is supposed to be. It is an hereditary aristocracy, assuming and asserting indefeasible, irrevocable rights and authority, wholly independent of the nation. Where then was the merited popularity of exalting this hereditary power over another hereditary power less independent of the nation than what itself assumed to be, and of absorbing the rights of the nation into a house over which it has neither election nor control?

The general impulse of the nation was right; but it acted without reflection. It approved the opposition made to the right set up by Mr. Fox, without perceiving that Mr. Pitt was supporting another indefeasible right more remote from the nation, in opposition to it.

With respect to the house of commons, it is elected but by a small part of the nation; but were the election as universal as taxation, which it ought to be, it would still be only the organ of the nation, and cannot possess inherent rights. When the national assembly of France resolves a matter, the resolve is made in right of the nation; but Mr. Pitt, on all national questions, so far as they refer to the house of commons, absorbs the right of the nation into the organ, and makes the organ into a nation, and the nation itself into a cipher.

In a few words, the question on the regency was a question on a million a year, which is appropriated to the executive department; and Mr. Pitt could not possess himself of any management of this sum without setting up the supremacy of parliament; and when this was accomplished, it was indifferent who should be regent, as he must be regent at his own cost. Among the curiosities which this contentious debate afforded was that of making the great seal into a king; the affixing of which to an act was to be royal authority. If, therefore, royal authority is a great seal, it consequently is in itself nothing; and a good constitution would be of infinitely more value to the nation than what the three nominal powers, as they now stand, are worth.

The continual use of the word *constitution* in the English parliament shows there is none, and that the whole is merely a form of government without a constitution, and constituting itself with what powers it pleases. If there was a constitution, it certainly would be referred to; and the debate on any constitutional point would terminate by producing the constitution. One member says, this is constitutional; another says, that is constitutional. Today it is one thing; tomorrow it is something else—while the maintaining the debate proves there is none. Constitution is now the cant word of parliament, turning itself to the ear of the nation. Formerly it was the *universal supremacy and the omnipotence of parliament.* But since the progress of liberty in France, those phrases have a despotic harshness in their note; and the English parliament has caught the fashion from the national assembly, but without the substance, of speaking of *a constitution.*

As the present generation of people in England did not make
the government, they are not accountable for any of its defects;
but that sooner or later it must come into their hands to undergo
a constitutional reformation is as certain as that the same thing
has happened in France. If France, with a revenue of nearly
twenty-four millions sterling, with an extent of rich and fertile
country above four times larger than England, with a population of twenty-four millions of inhabitants to support taxation,
with upwards of ninety millions sterling of gold and silver cir-
culating in the nation, and with a debt less than the present
debt of England, still found it necessary, from whatever cause,
to come to a settlement of its affairs, it solves the problem of
funding for both countries.

It is out of the question to say how long what is called the
English constitution has lasted and to argue from thence how
long it is to last; the question is how long can the funding system last? It is a thing but of modern invention and has not yet
continued beyond the life of a man; yet in that short space it has
so far accumulated, that, together with the current expenses, it
requires an amount of taxes at least equal to the whole landed
rental of the nation in acres to defray the annual expenditures.
That a government could not always have gone on by the same
system which has been followed for the last seventy years,
must be evident to every man; and for the same reason it cannot always go on.

The funding system is not money; neither is it, properly
speaking, credit. It, in effect, creates upon paper the sum which
it appears to borrow, and lays on a tax to keep the imaginary
capital alive by the payment of interest, and sends the annuity
to market to be sold for paper already in circulation. If any
credit is given, it is to the disposition of the people to pay the
tax, and not to the government which lays it on. When this
disposition expires, what is supposed to be the credit of government expires with it. The instance of France, under the former
government, shows that it is impossible to compel the payment
of taxes by force when a whole nation is determined to take its
stand upon that ground.

Mr. Burke, in his review of the finances of France, states the quantity of gold and silver in France at about eighty-eight millions sterling. In doing this he has, I presume, divided by the difference of exchange, instead of the standard of twenty-four livres to a pound sterling; for M. Neckar's statement, from which Mr. Burke's is taken, is *two thousand two hundred millions of livres*, which is upwards of ninety-one millions and a half sterling. . . .

That the quantity of money in France cannot be under this sum may at once be seen from the state of the French revenue, without referring to the records of the French mint for proofs. The revenue of France prior to the revolution was nearly twenty-four millions sterling; and as paper had then no existence in France, the whole revenue was collected upon gold and silver; and it would have been impossible to have collected such a quantity of revenue upon a less national quantity than M. Neckar has stated. Before the establishment of paper in England, the revenue was about a fourth part of the national amount of gold and silver, as may be known by referring to the revenue prior to King William, and the quantity of money stated to be in the nation at that time, which was nearly as much as it is now.

It can be of no real service to a nation to impose upon itself, or to permit itself to be imposed upon; but the prejudices of some and the imposition of others have always represented France as a nation possessing but little money, whereas the quantity is not only more than four times what the quantity is in England, but is considerably greater on a proportion of numbers. To account for this deficiency on the part of England, some reference should be had to the English system of funding. It operates to multiply paper, and to substitute it in the room of money in various shapes; and the more paper is multiplied, the more opportunities are afforded to export the specie; and it admits of a possibility (by extending it to small notes) of increasing paper, till there is no money left. . . .

Lisbon and Cadiz are the two ports into which (money) gold and silver from South America are imported, and which afterwards divides and spreads itself over Europe by means of commerce, and increases the quantity of money in all parts of Europe. If, therefore, the amount of the annual importation into Europe can be known, and the relative proportion of the foreign commerce of the several nations by which it is distributed can be ascertained, they give a rule, sufficiently true, to ascertain the quantity of money which ought to be found in any nation at any given time.

M. Neckar shows from the registers of Lisbon and Cadiz that the importation of gold and silver into Europe is five millions sterling annually. He has not taken it on a single year, but on an average of fifteen succeeding years, from 1763 to 1777, both inclusive; in which time the amount was one thousand eight hundred million livres, which is seventy-five millions sterling.

From the commencement of the Hanover succession in 1714, to the time Mr. Chalmers published, is seventy-two years; and the quantity imported into Europe in that time would be three hundred and sixty millions sterling.

If the foreign commerce of Great Britain be stated at a sixth part of what the whole foreign commerce of Europe amounts to (which is probably an inferior estimation to what the gentlemen at the exchange would allow), the proportion which Britain should draw by commerce, of this sum, to keep herself on a proportion with the rest of Europe, would be also a sixth part, which is sixty millions sterling; and if the same allowance for waste and accident be made for England, which M. Neckar makes for France, the quantity remaining after these deductions would be fifty-two millions . . .; instead of which there were but twenty millions, which is forty-six millions below its proportionate quantity.

As the quantity of gold and silver imported into Lisbon and Cadiz is more easily ascertained than that of any commodity imported into England; and as the quantity of money coined at the Tower of London is still more positively known, the leading facts do not admit of a controversy. Either, therefore, the Commerce of England is unproductive of profit, or the gold and silver which it brings in, leak continually away by unseen means at the average rate of about three quarters of a million a year, which in the course of seventy-two years accounts for the deficiency; and its absence is supplied by paper.[1]

[1]Whether the English commerce does not bring in money, or whether the government sends it out after it is brought in, is a matter which the parties concerned can best explain; but that the deficiency exists is not in the power of either to disprove. While Dr. Price, Mr. Eden (now Auckland), Mr. Chalmers, and others were debating whether the quantity of money was greater or less than at the revolution, the circumstance was not adverted to that since the revolution there cannot have been less than four hundred millions sterling imported into Europe; and therefore the quantity in England ought at least to have been four times greater than it was at the revolution, to be on a proportion with Europe. What England is now doing by paper is what she should have been able to do by solid money, if gold and silver had come into the nation in the proportion it ought, or had not been sent out; and she is endeavoring to restore by paper, the balance she has lost by money. It is certain that the gold and silver which arrive annually in the register-ships to Spain and Portugal do not remain in those countries. Taking the value half in gold and half in silver, it is about four hundred tons annually; and from the number of ships and galleons employed in the trade of bringing those metals from South America to Portugal and Spain, the quantity sufficiently proves itself, without referring to the registers.

In the situation England now is, it is impossible she can increase in money. High taxes not only lessen the property of the individuals, but they lessen also the money capital of the nation, by inducing smuggling, which can only be carried on by gold and silver. By the politics which the British government have carried on with the inland powers of Germany and the continent, it has made an enemy of all the maritime powers, and is therefore obliged to keep up a large navy; but though the navy is built in England, the naval stores must be purchased from abroad, and that from countries where the greatest part must be paid for in gold and silver. Some fallacious rumors have been set afloat in England to induce a belief of money, and, among others, that of the French refugees bringing great quantities. The idea is ridiculous. The general part of the money in France is silver; and it would take upwards of twenty of the largest broad-wheel wagons, with ten horses each, to remove one million sterling of silver. Is it then to be supposed that a few people fleeing on horseback or in post-chaises, in a secret manner, and having the French custom-house to pass, and the sea to cross, could bring even a sufficiency for their own expenses?

The revolution of France is attended with many novel circumstances, not only in the political sphere, but in the circle of money transactions. Among others, it shows that a government may be in a state of insolvency, and a nation rich. So far as the fact is confined to the late government of France, it was insolvent; because the nation would no longer support its extravagance, and therefore it could no longer support itself—but with respect to the nation all the means existed. A government may be said to be insolvent every time it applies to a nation to discharge its arrears. The insolvency of the late government of France, and the present government of England, differed in no other respect than as the disposition of the people differ. The people of France refused their aid to the old government, and the people of England submit to taxation without inquiry. What is called the crown in England has been insolvent several times; the last of which, publicly known, was in May, 1777, when it applied to the nation to discharge upwards of £600,000 private debts, which otherwise it could not pay.

It was the error of Mr. Pitt, Mr. Burke, and all those who were unacquainted with the affairs of France to confound the French nation with the French government. The French nation, in effect, endeavored to render the late government insolvent, for the purpose of taking government into its own hands; and it reserved its means for the support of the new government. In a country of such vast extent and population as France, the natural means cannot be wanting; and the political means appear the instant the nation is disposed to permit them. When Mr. Burke, in a speech last winter in the British parliament, *cast his eyes over*

When millions of money are spoken of, it should be recollected, that such sums can only accumulate in a country by slow degrees and a long procession of time. The most frugal system that England could now adopt would not recover in a century the balance she has lost in money since the commencement of the Hanover succession. She is seventy millions behind France, and she must be, in some considerable proportion, behind every country in Europe, because the returns of the English mint do not show an increase of money, while the registers of Lisbon and Cadiz show a European increase of between three and four hundred millions sterling.

the map of Europe, and saw a chasm that once was France,
he talked like a dreamer of dreams. The same natural
France existed as before, and all the natural means existed
with it. The only chasm was that which the extinction of
despotism had left, and which was to be filled up with a constitution more formidable in resources than the power which had
expired.

Although the French nation rendered the late government
insolvent, it did not permit the insolvency to act towards the
creditors; and the creditors, considering the nation as the real
paymaster and the government only as the agent, rested themselves on the nation in preference to the government. This
appears greatly to disturb Mr. Burke, as the precedent is fatal to
the policy by which governments have supposed themselves
secure. They have contracted debts with a view of attaching
what is called the moneyed interest of a nation to their support;
but the example in France shows that the permanent security of
the creditor is in the nation, and not in the government; and that
in all possible revolutions that may happen in governments, the
means are always with the nation, and the nation always in existence. Mr. Burke argues that the creditors ought to have
abided the fate of the government which they trusted; but the
national assembly considered them as the creditors of the nation, not of the government—of the master, and not of the
steward.

Notwithstanding the late government could not discharge
the current expenses, the present government has paid off a
great part of the capital. This has been accomplished by two
means; the one by lessening the expenses of government, and
the other by the sale of the monastic and ecclesiastical landed
estates. The devotees and penitent debauchees, extortioners
and misers of former days, to ensure themselves a better world
than that they were about to leave, had bequeathed immense
property in trust to the priesthood for *pious uses;* and the priesthood kept it for themselves. The national assembly has ordered
it to be sold for the good of the whole nation, and the priesthood
to be decently provided for.

In consequence of the revolution, the annual interest of the debt of France will be reduced at least six millions sterling, by paying off upwards of one hundred millions of the capital; which, with lessening the former expenses of government at least three millions, will place France in a situation worthy the imitation of Europe.

Upon a whole review of the subject, how vast is the contrast! While Mr. Burke has been talking of a general bankruptcy in France, the national assembly have been paying off the capital of the national debt; and while taxes have increased nearly a million a year in England, they have lowered several millions a year in France. Not a word has either Mr. Burke or Mr. Pitt said about French affairs, or the state of the French finances, in the present session of parliament. The subject begins to be too well understood, and imposition serves no longer.

There is a general enigma running through the whole of Mr. Burke's book. He writes in a rage against the national assembly: but what is he enraged about? If his assertions were as true as they are groundless, and if France, by her revolution, had annihilated her power and become what he calls a *chasm*, it might excite the grief of a Frenchman (considering himself as a national man), and provoke his rage against the national assembly; but why should it excite the rage of Mr. Burke? Alas! it is not the nation of France that Mr. Burke means, but the *court;* and every court in Europe, dreading the same fate, is in mourning. He writes neither in the character of a Frenchman nor an Englishman, but in the fawning character of that creature, known in all countries as a friend to none, a *courtier.* Whether it be the court of Versailles, or the court of St. James, or of Carlton House, or the court in expectation, signifies not; for the caterpillar principles of all courts and courtiers are alike. They form a common policy throughout Europe, detached and separate from the interest of the nations, and while they appear to quarrel, they agree to plunder. Nothing can be more terrible to a court or courtier than the revolution of France. That which is a blessing to nations, is bitterness to them; and, as their existence depends on the duplicity of a country, they tremble at the approach of principles, and dread the precedent that threatens their overthrow.

CONCLUSION [TO PART I]

Reason and ignorance, the opposites of each other, influence the great bulk of mankind. If either of these can be rendered sufficiently extensive in a country, the machinery of government goes easily on. Reason shows itself, and ignorance submits to whatever is dictated to it.

The two modes of government which prevail in the world, are, 1st, government by election and representation; 2d, government by hereditary succession. The former is generally known by the name of republic; the latter by that of monarchy and aristocracy.

Those two distinct and opposite forms erect themselves on the two distinct and opposite bases of reason and ignorance. As the exercise of government requires talents and abilities, and as talents and abilities cannot have hereditary descent, it is evident that hereditary succession requires a belief from man to which his reason cannot subscribe, and which can only be established upon his ignorance; and the more ignorant any country is, the better it is fitted for this species of government.

On the contrary, government in a well-constituted republic, requires no belief from man beyond what his reason authorizes. He sees the *rationale* of the whole system, its origin and its operation; and as it is best supported when best understood, the human faculties act with boldness and acquire, under this form of government, a gigantic manliness.

As, therefore, each of those forms acts on a different basis, the one moving freely by the aid of reason, the other by ignorance; we have next to consider what it is that gives motion to that species of government which is called mixed government, or, as it is sometimes ludicrously styled, a government of *this, that, and t'other.*

The moving power in this species of government is, of necessity, corruption. However imperfect election and representation may be in mixed governments, they still give exertion to a greater portion of reason than is convenient to the hereditary part; and therefore it becomes necessary to buy the reason up. A mixed government is an imperfect everything, cementing and soldering the discordant parts together by corruption, to act as a whole. Mr. Burke appears highly disgusted that France, since she had resolved on a revolution, did not adopt what he calls "a British constitution"; and the regret which he expresses on this occasion implies a suspicion that the British constitution needed something to keep its defects in countenance.

In mixed governments there is no responsibility; the parts cover each other till responsibility is lost; and the corruption which moves the machine contrives at the same time its own escape. When it is laid down as a maxim that *a king can do no wrong*, it places him in a state of similar security with that of idiots and persons insane, and responsibility is out of the question with respect to himself. It then descends upon the minister who shelters himself under a majority in parliament which, by places, pensions, and corruption, he can always command; and that majority justifies itself by the same authority with which it protects the minister. In this rotatory motion, responsibility is thrown off from the parts and from the whole.

When there is a part in a government which can do no wrong, it implies that it does nothing; and is only the machine of another power, by whose advice and direction it acts. What is supposed to be the king, in mixed governments, is the cabinet; and as the cabinet is always a part of the parliament, and the members justifying in one character what they act in another, a mixed government becomes a continual enigma; entailing upon a country, by the quantity of corruption necessary to solder the parts, the expense of supporting all the forms of government at once, and finally resolving itself into a government by committee; in which the advisers, the actors, the approvers, the justifiers, the persons responsible, and the persons not responsible, are the same persons.

By this pantomimical contrivance and change of scene and character, the parts help each other out in matters which neither of them singly would presume to act. When money is to be obtained, the mass of variety apparently dissolves, and a profusion of parliamentary praises passes between the parts. Each admires, with astonishment, the wisdom, the liberality, and disinterestedness of the other; and all of them breathe a pitying sigh at the burdens of the nation.

But in a well-conditioned republic, nothing of this soldering, praising, and pitying, can take place; the representation being equal throughout the country and complete in itself, however it may be arranged into legislative and executive, they have all one and the same natural source. The parts are not foreigners to each other, like democracy, aristocracy, and monarchy. As there are no discordant distinctions, there is nothing to corrupt by compromise or confound by contrivance. Public measures appeal of themselves to the understanding of the nation, and resting on their own merits, disown any flattering application to vanity. The continual whine of lamenting the burden of taxes, however successfully it may be practiced in mixed governments, is inconsistent with the sense and spirit of a republic. If taxes are necessary, they are of course advantageous; but if they require an apology, the apology itself implies an impeachment. Why then is man thus imposed upon, or why does he impose upon himself?

When men are spoken of as kings and subjects, or when government is mentioned under distinct or combined heads of monarchy, aristocracy, and democracy, what is it that *reasoning* man is to understand by the terms? If there really existed in the world two more distinct and separate *elements* of human power, we should then see the several origins to which those terms would descriptively apply: but as there is but one species of man, there can be but one element of human power, and that element is man himself. Monarchy, aristocracy, and democracy are but creatures of imagination; and a thousand such may be contrived as well as three.

From the revolutions of America and France and the symptoms that have appeared in other countries, it is evident that the opinion of the world is changing with respect to systems of government, and that revolutions are not within the compass of political calculations. The progress of time and circumstances, which men assign to the accomplishment of great changes, is too mechanical to measure the force of the mind and the rapidity of reflection by which revolutions are generated; all the old governments have received a shock from those that already appear, and which were once more improbable, and are a greater subject of wonder, than a general revolution in Europe would be now.

When we survey the wretched condition of man under the monarchical and hereditary systems of government, dragged from his home by one power, or driven by another, and impoverished by taxes more than by enemies, it becomes evident that those systems are bad, and that a general revolution in the principle and construction of governments is necessary.

What is government more than the management of the affairs of a nation? It is not, and from its nature cannot be, the property of any particular man or family, but of the whole community at whose expense it is supported; and though by force or contrivance it has been usurped into an inheritance, the usurpation cannot alter the right of things. Sovereignty, as a matter of right, appertains to the nation only and not to any individual; and a nation has at all times an inherent, indefeasible right to abolish any form of government it finds inconvenient, and establish such as accords with its interest, disposition, and happiness. The romantic and barbarous distinctions of men into kings and subjects, though it may suit the condition of courtiers cannot that of citizens; and is exploded by the principle upon which governments are now founded. Every citizen is a member of the sovereignty, and as such can acknowledge no personal subjection; and his obedience can be only to the laws.

When men think of what government is, they must necessarily suppose it to possess a knowledge of all the objects and matters upon which its authority is to be exercised. In this view of government, the republican system, as established by America and France, operates to embrace the whole of a nation; and the knowledge necessary to the interest of all the parts is to be found in the center, which the parts by representation form: but the old governments are on a construction that excludes knowledge as well as happiness; government by monks, who know nothing of the world beyond the walls of a convent, is as consistent as government by kings.

What were formerly called revolutions were little more than a change of persons or an alteration of local circumstances. They rose and fell like things of course, and had nothing in their existence or their fate that could influence beyond the spot that produced them. But what we now see in the world, from the revolutions of America and France, are a renovation of the natural order of things, a system of principles as universal as truth and the existence of man, and combining moral with political happiness and national prosperity.

"I. Men are born and always continue free and equal in respect to their rights. Civil distinctions, therefore, can be founded only on public utility.

"II. The end of all political associations is the preservation of the natural and imprescriptible rights of man, and these rights are liberty, property, security and resistance of oppression.

"III. The nation is essentially the source of all sovereignty; nor can any individual, or any body of men, be entitled to any authority which is not expressly derived from it."

In these principles there is nothing to throw a nation into confusion by inflaming ambition. They are calculated to call forth wisdom and abilities, and to exercise them for the public good and not for the emolument or aggrandizement of particular descriptions of men or families. Monarchical sovereignty, the enemy of mankind and the source of misery, is abolished; and sovereignty itself is restored to its natural and original place, the nation. Were this the case throughout Europe, the cause of wars would be taken away.

It is attributed to Henry IV of France, a man of an enlarged and benevolent heart, that he proposed about the year 1620 a plan for abolishing war in Europe. The plan consisted in constituting a European congress or, as the French authors style it, a pacific republic; by appointing delegates from the several nations, who were to act as a court of arbitration in any disputes that might arise between nation and nation.

Had such a plan been adopted at the time it was proposed, the taxes of England and France, as two of the parties, would have been at least ten millions sterling annually, to each nation, less than they were at the commencement of the French revolution.

To conceive a cause why such a plan has not been adopted (and that instead of a congress for the purpose of preventing war, it has been called only to *terminate* a war after a fruitless expense of several years) it will be necessary to consider the interest of governments as a distinct interest to that of nations.

Whatever is the cause of taxes to a nation becomes also the means of revenue to a government. Every war terminates with an addition of taxes, and consequently with an addition of revenue; and in any event of war, in the manner they are now commenced and concluded, the power and interest of governments are increased. War, therefore, from its productiveness, as it easily furnishes the pretense of necessity for taxes and appointments to places and offices, becomes the principal part of the system of old governments; and to establish any mode to abolish war, however advantageous it might be to nations, would be to take from such government the most lucrative of its branches. The frivolous matters upon which war is made show the disposition and avidity of governments to uphold the system of war, and betray the motives upon which they act.

Why are not republics plunged into war, but because the nature of their government does not admit of an interest distinct from that of the nation? Even Holland, though an ill-constructed republic, and with a commerce extending over the world, existed nearly a century without war; and the instant the form of government was changed in France, the republican principles of peace and domestic prosperity and economy arose with the new government; and the same consequences would follow the same causes in other nations.

As war is the system of government on the old construction, the animosity which nations reciprocally entertain, is nothing more than what the policy of their governments excite to keep up the spirit of the system. Each government accuses the other of perfidy, intrigue, and ambition as a means of heating the imagination of their respective nations, and incensing them to hostilities. Man is not the enemy of man, but through the medium of a false system of government. Instead therefore of exclaiming against the ambition of kings, the exclamation should be directed against the principle of such governments; and instead of seeking to reform the individual, the wisdom of a nation should apply itself to reform the system.

Whether the forms and maxims of governments which are still in practice were adapted to the condition of the world at the period they were established is not in this case the question. The older they are the less correspondence can they have with the present state of things. Time and change of circumstances and opinions have the same progressive effect in rendering modes of government obsolete, as they have upon customs and manners. Agriculture, commerce, manufactures, and the tranquil arts, by which the prosperity of nations is best promoted, require a different system of government and a different species of knowledge to direct its operations, to what might have been the former condition of the world.

As it is not difficult to perceive, from the enlightened state of mankind, that hereditary governments are verging to their decline and that revolutions on the broad basis of national sovereignty, and government by representation, are making their way in Europe, it would be an act of wisdom to anticipate their approach and produce revolutions by reason and accommodation, rather than commit them to the issue of convulsions.

From what we now see, nothing of reform in the political world ought to be held improbable. It is an age of revolutions in which everything may be looked for. The intrigue of courts, by which the system of war is kept up, may provoke a confederation of nations to abolish it; and a European congress to patronize the progress of free government and promote the civilization of nations with each other is an event nearer in probability than once were the revolutions and alliance of France and America.

PART II

[DEDICATION]

To M. de la Fayette

After an acquaintance of nearly fifteen years in difficult situations in America and various consultations in Europe, I feel a pleasure in presenting you this small treatise in gratitude for your services to my beloved America, and as a testimony of my esteem for the virtues, public and private, which I know you to possess.

The only point upon which I could ever discover that we differed was not as to principles of government, but as to time. For my own part, I think it equally as injurious to good principles to permit them to linger as to push them on too fast. That which you suppose accomplishable in fourteen or fifteen years, I may believe practicable in a much shorter period. Mankind, as it appears to me, are always ripe enough to understand their true interest, provided it be presented clearly to their understanding, and that in a manner not to create suspicion by anything like self-design, nor to offend by assuming too much. Where we would wish to reform we must not reproach.

When the American Revolution was established I felt a disposition to sit serenely down and enjoy the calm. It did not appear to me that any object could afterwards arise great enough to make me quit tranquillity and feel as I had felt before. But when principle, and not place, is the energetic cause of action, a man, I find, is everywhere the same.

I am now once more in the public world; and as I have not a right to contemplate on so many years of remaining life as you have, I am resolved to labor as fast as I can; and as I am anxious for your aid and your company, I wish you to hasten your principles and overtake me.

If you make a campaign the ensuing spring, which it is most probable there will be no occasion for, I will come and join you.

Should the campaign commence, I hope it will terminate in the extinction of German despotism and in establishing the freedom of all Germany. When France shall be surrounded with revolutions, she will be in peace and safety and her taxes, as well as those of Germany, will consequently become less.

Your sincere,

Affectionate friend,

THOMAS PAINE

London, Feb. 9, 1792

PREFACE

When I began the chapter entitled the *Conclusion*, in the former part of *The Rights of Man,* published last year, it was my intention to have extended it to a greater length; but in casting the whole matter in my mind which I wished to add, I found that I must either make the work too bulky or contract my plan too much. I therefore brought it to a close as soon as the subject would admit, and reserved what I had further to say to another opportunity.

Several other reasons contributed to produce this determination. I wished to know the manner in which a work, written in a style of thinking and expression at variance with what had been customary in England, would be received before I proceeded further. A great field was opening to the view of mankind by means of the French revolution. Mr. Burke's outrageous opposition thereto brought the controversy into England. He attacked principles which he knew (from information) I would contest with him, because they are principles I believe to be good and which I have contributed to establish and conceive myself bound to defend. Had he not urged the controversy, I had most probably been a silent man.

Another reason for deferring the remainder of the work was that Mr. Burke promised in his first publication to renew the subject at another opportunity and to make a comparison of what he called the English and French consitutions. I therefore held myself in reserve for him. He has published two works since without doing this; which he certainly would not have omitted had the comparison been in his favor.

In his last work, his "Appeal from the New to the Old Whigs," he has quoted about ten pages from *The Rights of Man*, and having given himself the trouble of doing this, says, "he shall not attempt in the smallest degree to refute them," meaning the principles therein contained. I am enough acquainted with Mr. Burke to know that he would if he could. But instead of contesting them, he immediately after consoles himself with saying that "he has done his part." He has not done his part. He has not performed his promise of a comparison of constitutions. He started a controversy, he gave the challenge, and has fled from it; and he is now a *case in point* with his own opinion that *"the age of chivalry is gone!"*

The title, as well as the substance of his last work, his Appeal, is his condemnation. Principles must rest on their own merits, and if they are good they certainly will. To put them under the shelter of other men's authority, as Mr. Burke has done, serves to bring them into suspicion. Mr. Burke is not very fond of dividing his honors, but in this case he is artfully dividing the disgrace.

But who are those to whom Mr. Burke has appealed? A set of childish thinkers and half-way politicians born in the last century; men who went no further with any principle than as it suited their purpose as a party; the nation sees nothing in such works or such politics worthy its attention. A little matter will move a party, but it must be something great that moves a nation.

Though I see nothing in Mr. Burke's Appeal worth taking notice of, there is, however, one expression upon which I shall offer a few remarks.—After quoting largely from the *Rights of Man*, and declining to contest the principles contained in that work, he says, "This will most probably be done (*if such writings shall be thought to deserve any other refutation than that of criminal justice*) by others, who may think with Mr. Burke and with the same zeal."

In the first place, it has not been done by anybody. Not less, I believe, than eight or ten pamphlets, intended as answers to the former part of the *Rights of Man* have been published by different persons, and not one of them, to my knowledge, has extended to a second edition, nor are even the titles of them so much as generally remembered. As I am averse to unnecessarily multiplying publications, I have answered none of them. And as I believe that a man may write himself out of reputation when nobody else can do it, I am careful to avoid that rock.

But as I decline unnecessary publications on the one hand, so would I avoid anything that looked like sullen pride on the other. If Mr. Burke, or any person on his side the question, will produce an answer to the *Rights of Man* that shall extend to a half or even a fourth part of the number of copies to which the *Rights of Man* extended, I will reply to his work. But until this be done, I shall so far take the sense of the public for my guide (and the world knows I am not a flatterer) that what they do not think worth while to read, is not worth mine to answer. I suppose the number of copies to which the first part of the *Rights of Man* extended, taking England, Scotland, and Ireland, is not less than between forty and fifty thousand.

I now come to remark on the remaining part of the quotation I have made from Mr. Burke.

"If," says he, "such writings shall be thought to deserve any other refutation than that of *criminal* justice."

Pardoning the pun, it must be *criminal* justice indeed that should condemn a work as a substitute for not being able to refute it. The greatest condemnation that could be passed upon it would be a refutation. But, in proceeding by the method Mr. Burke alludes to, the condemnation would in the final event pass upon the criminality of the process and not upon the work, and in this case I had rather be the author than be either the judge or the jury that should condemn it.

But to come at once to the point. I have differed from some professional gentlemen on the subject of prosecutions, and I since find they are falling into my opinion, which I shall here state as fully, but as concisely as I can.

I will first put a case with respect to any law, and then compare it with a government, or with what in England is, or has
been, called a constitution.

It would be an act of despotism, or what in England is
called arbitrary power, to make a law to prohibit investigating
the principles, good or bad, on which such a law or any other
is founded.

If a law be bad, it is one thing to oppose the practice of it, but
it is quite a different thing to expose its errors, to reason on its
defects, and to show cause why it should be repealed, or why
another ought to be substituted in its place. I have always held
it an opinion (making it also my practice) that it is better to obey
a bad law, making use at the same time of every argument to
show its errors and procure its repeal, than forcibly to violate it;
because the precedent of breaking a bad law might weaken the
force, and lead to a discretionary violation, of those which are
good.

The case is the same with respect to principles and forms of
government, or to what are called constitutions, and the parts
of which they are composed.

It is for the good of nations and not for the emolument or aggrandizement of particular individuals that government ought
to be established, and that mankind are at the expense of supporting it. The defects of every government and constitution
both as to principle and form, must, on a parity of reasoning, be
as open to discussion as the defects of a law, and it is a duty
which every man owes to society to point them out. When
those defects and the means of remedying them are generally
seen by a nation, that nation will reform its government or its
constitution in the one case, as the government repealed or reformed the law in the other. The operation of government is
restricted to the making and the administering of laws; but it is
to a nation that the rights of forming or reforming, generating
or regenerating constitutions and governments belong; and consequently those subjects, as subjects of investigation, are always
before a country *as a matter of right*, and cannot, without in-
vading the general rights of that country, be made subjects for

prosecution. On this ground I will meet Mr. Burke whenever he pleases. It is better that the whole argument should come out than to seek to stifle it. It was himself that opened the controversy, and he ought not to desert it.

I do not believe that monarchy and aristocracy will continue seven years longer in any of the enlightened countries of Europe. If better reasons can be shown for them than against them, they will stand; if the contrary, they will not. Mankind are not now to be told they shall not think, or they shall not read: and publications that go no further than to investigate principles of government, to invite men to reason and to reflect, and to show the errors and excellencies of different systems, have a right to appear. If they do not excite attention, they are not worth the trouble of a prosecution; and if they do the prosecution will amount to nothing, since it cannot amount to a prohibition of reading. This would be a sentence on the public, instead of the author, and would also be the most effectual mode of making or hastening revolutions.

On all cases that apply universally to a nation, with respect to systems of government, a jury of *twelve* men is not competent to decide. Where there are no witnesses to be examined, no facts to be proved, and where the whole matter is before the whole public, and the merits or demerits of it resting on their opinion; and where there is nothing to be known in a court, but what everybody knows out of it, every twelve men are equally as good a jury as the other and would most probably reverse each other's verdict; or from the variety of their opinions, not be able to form one. It is one case whether a nation approve a work or a plan; but it is quite another case whether it will commit to any such jury the power of determining whether that nation has a right to, or shall reform its government, or not. I mention these cases that Mr. Burke may see I have not written on government without reflecting on what is law, as well as on what are rights. The only effectual jury in such cases would be a convention of the whole nation fairly elected; for in all such cases the whole nation is the vicinage.

As to the prejudices which men have from education and

habit in favor of any particular form or system of government, those prejudices have yet to stand the test of reason and reflection. In fact such prejudices are nothing. No man is prejudiced in favor of a thing knowing it to be wrong. He is attached to it on the belief of its being right; and when he sees it is not so, the prejudice will be gone. We have but a defective idea of what prejudice is. It might be said that until men think for themselves the whole is prejudice and *not opinion;* for that only is opinion which is the result of reason and reflection. I offer this remark, that Mr. Burke may not confide too much in what has been the customary prejudices of the country.

But admitting governments to be changed all over Europe, it certainly may be done without convulsion or revenge. It is not worth making changes or revolutions, unless it be for some great national benefit, and when this shall appear to a nation the danger will be, as in America and France, to those who oppose; and with this reflection I close my preface.

THOMAS PAINE

London, Feb. 9, 1792

INTRODUCTION

What Archimedes said of the mechanical powers, may be applied to reason and liberty: *"Had we,"* said he, *"a place to stand upon, we might raise the world."*

The revolution in America presented in politics what was only theory in mechanics. So deeply rooted were all the governments of the old world, and so effectually had the tyranny and the antiquity of habit established itself over the mind, that no beginning could be made in Asia, Africa, or Europe, to reform the political condition of man. Freedom had been hunted round the globe; reason was considered as rebellion; and the slavery of fear had made men afraid to think.

But such is the irresistible nature of truth that all it asks, and all it wants, is the liberty of appearing. The sun needs no inscription to distinguish him from darkness, and no sooner did the

American governments display themselves to the world than despotism felt a shock and man began to contemplate redress.

The independence of America, considered merely as a separation from England, would have been a matter but of little importance had it not been accompanied by a revolution in the principles and practice of government. She made a stand, not for herself only, but for the world, and looked beyond the advantages which *she* could receive. Even the Hessian, though hired to fight against her, may live to bless his defeat; and England, condemning the viciousness of its government, rejoice in its miscarriage.

As America was the only spot in the political world where the principles of universal reformation could begin, so also was it the best in the natural world. An assemblage of circumstances conspired not only to give birth but to add gigantic maturity to its principles. The scene which that country presents to the eye of the spectator has something in it which generates and enlarges great ideas. Nature appears to him in magnitude. The mighty objects he beholds act upon his mind by enlarging it, and he partakes of the greatness he contemplates. Its first settlers were emigrants from different European nations, and of diversified professions of religion, retiring from the governmental persecutions of the old world, and meeting in the new not as enemies but as brothers. The wants which necessarily accompany the cultivation of a wilderness produced among them a state of society which countries long harassed by the quarrels and intrigues of governments had neglected to cherish. In such a situation man becomes what he ought to be. He sees his species not with the inhuman idea of a natural enemy but as kindred; and the example shows to the artificial world that man must go back to nature for information.

From the rapid progress which America makes in every species of improvement, it is rational to conclude that if the governments of Asia, Africa and Europe had begun on a principle similar to that of America, or had they not been very early corrupted therefrom, those countries must by this time have been in a far superior condition to what they are. Age after age has passed away for no other purpose than to behold their wretchedness. Could we suppose a spectator who knew nothing of the world and who was put into it merely to make his observations, he would take a great part of the old world to be new, just struggling with the difficulties and hardships of an infant settlement. He could not suppose that the hordes of miserable poor, with which old countries abound, could be any other than those who had not yet been able to provide for themselves. Little would he think they were the consequence of what in such countries is called government.

If, from the more wretched parts of the old world, we look at those which are in an advanced state of improvement, we still find the greedy hand of government thrusting itself into every corner and crevice of industry, and grasping the spoil of the multitude. Invention is continually exercised to furnish new pretenses for revenue and taxation. It watches prosperity as its prey, and permits none to escape without a tribute.

As revolutions have begun (and as the probability is always greater against a thing beginning, than of proceeding after it has begun), it is natural to expect that other revolutions will follow. The amazing and still increasing expenses with which old governments are conducted, the numerous wars they engage in or provoke, the embarrassments they throw in the way of universal civilization and commerce, and the oppression and usurpation acted at home, have wearied out the patience and exhausted the property of the world. In such a situation, and with such examples already existing, revolutions are to be looked for. They are become subjects of universal conversation, and may be considered as the *order of the day*.

If systems of government can be introduced less expensive and more productive of general happiness than those which have existed, all attempts to oppose their progress will in the end prove fruitless. Reason, like time, will make its own way, and prejudice will fall in the combat with interest. If universal peace, harmony, civilization, and commerce are ever to be the happy lot of man, it cannot be accomplished but by a revolution in the present system of governments. All the monarchical governments are military. War is their trade, plunder and revenue their objects. While such governments continue, peace has not the absolute security of a day. What is the history of all monarchical governments but a disgustful picture of human wretchedness, and the accidental respite of a few years repose? Wearied with war, and tired with human butchery, they sat down to rest and called it peace. This certainly is not the condition that heaven intended for man; and if *this be monarchy*, well might monarchy be reckoned among the sins of the Jews.

The revolutions which formerly took place in the world had nothing in them that interested the bulk of mankind. They extended only to a change of persons and measures but not of principles, and rose or fell among the common transactions of the moment. What we now behold may not improperly be called a "*counter revolution.*" Conquest and tyranny, at some early period, dispossessed man of his rights, and he is now recovering them. And as the tide of human affairs has its ebb and flow in directions contrary to each other, so also is it in this. Government founded on a *moral theory, on a system of universal peace, on the indefeasible, hereditary rights of man,* is now revolving from west to east by a stronger impulse than the government of the sword revolved from east to west. It interests not particular individuals but nations in its progress, and promises a new era to the human race.

The danger to which the success of revolutions is most exposed is that of attempting them before the principles on which they proceed, and the advantages to result from them, are sufficiently understood. Almost everything appertaining to the circumstances of a nation has been absorbed and confounded under the general and mysterious word *government.* Though it avoids taking to its account the errors it commits and the mischiefs it occasions, it fails not to arrogate to itself whatever has the appearance of prosperity. It robs industry of its honors by pedantically making itself the cause of its effects; and purloins from the general character of man the merits that appertain to him as a social being.

It may therefore be of use, in this day of revolutions, to discriminate between those things which are the effect of government, and those which are not. This will best be done by taking a review of society and civilization, and the consequences resulting therefrom, as things distinct from what are called governments. By beginning with this investigation, we shall be able to assign effects to their proper causes, and analyze the mass of common errors.

CHAPTER I. OF SOCIETY AND CIVILIZATION

A great part of that order which reigns among mankind is not the effect of government. It had its origin in the principles of society and the natural constitution of man. It existed prior to government, and would exist if the formality of government was abolished. The mutual dependence and reciprocal interest which man has in man, and all the parts of a civilized community upon each other, create that great chain of connection which holds it together. The landholder, the farmer, the manufacturer, the merchant, the tradesman, and every occupation prospers by the aid which each receives from the other, and from the whole. Common interest regulates their concerns and forms their laws; and the laws which common usage ordains have a greater influence than the laws of government. In fine, society performs for itself almost everything which is ascribed to government.

To understand the nature and quantity of government proper for man, it is necessary to attend to his character. As nature created him for social life, she fitted him for the station she intended. In all cases she made his natural wants greater than his individual powers. No one man is capable, without the aid of society, of supplying his own wants; and those wants, acting upon every individual, impel the whole of them into society as naturally as gravitation acts to a center.

But she has gone further. She has not only forced man into society by a diversity of wants, which the reciprocal aid of each other can supply, but she has implanted in him a system of social affections, which, though not necessary to his existence, are essential to his happiness. There is no period in life when this love for society ceases to act. It begins and ends with our being.

If we examine with attention into the composition and constitution of man, the diversity of his wants, and the diversity of talents in different men for reciprocally accommodating the wants of each other, his propensity to society, and consequently to preserve the advantages resulting from it, we shall easily discover that a great part of what is called government is mere imposition.

Government is no further necessary than to supply the few cases to which society and civilization are not conveniently competent; and instances are not wanting to show that everything which government can usefully add thereto, has been performed by the common consent of society, without government.

For upwards of two years from the commencement of the American war, and a longer period in several of the American states, there were no established forms of government. The old governments had been abolished, and the country was too much occupied in defense to employ its attention in establishing new governments; yet during this interval order and harmony were preserved as inviolate as in any country in Europe. There is a natural aptness in man, and more so in society, because it embraces a greater variety of abilities and resources to accommodate itself to whatever situation it is in. The instant formal government is abolished, society begins to act. A general association takes place, and common interest produces common security.

So far is it from being true, as has been pretended, that the abolition of any formal government is the dissolution of society, it acts by a contrary impulse, and brings the latter the closer together. All that part of its organization which it had committed to its government devolves again upon itself, and acts through its medium. When men, as well from natural instinct as from reciprocal benefits, have habituated themselves to social and civilized life, there is always enough of its principles in practice to carry them through any changes they may find necessary or convenient to make in their government. In short, man is so naturally a creature of society, that it is almost impossible to put him out of it.

Formal government makes but a small part of civilized life; and when even the best that human wisdom can devise is established, it is a thing more in name and idea than in fact. It is to the great and fundamental principles of society and civilization—to the common usage universally consented to, and mutually and reciprocally maintained—to the unceasing circulation of interest, which, passing through its innumerable channels, invigorates the whole mass of civilized man—it is to these things, infinitely more than to anything which even the best instituted government can perform, that the safety and prosperity of the individual and of the whole depends.

The more perfect civilization is, the less occasion has it for government, because the more does it regulate its own affairs and govern itself; but so contrary is the practice of old governments to the reason of the case, that the expenses of them increase in the proportion they ought to diminish. It is but few general laws that civilized life requires, and those of such common usefulness, that whether they are enforced by the forms of government or not, the effect will be nearly the same. If we consider what the principles are that first condense men into society, and what the motives that regulate their mutual intercourse afterwards, we shall find, by the time we arrive at what is called government, that nearly the whole of the business is performed by the natural operation of the parts upon each other.

Man, with respect to all those matters, is more a creature of consistency than he is aware of, or than governments would wish him to believe. All the great laws of society are laws of nature. Those of trade and commerce, whether with respect to the intercourse of individuals or of nations, are laws of mutual and reciprocal interest. They are followed and obeyed, because it is the interest of the parties so to do, and not on account of any formal laws their governments may impose or interpose.

But how often is the natural propensity to society disturbed or destroyed by the operations of government! When the latter, instead of being ingrafted on the principles of the former, assumes to exist for itself, and acts by partialities of favor and oppression, it becomes the cause of the mischiefs it ought to prevent.

If we look back to the riots and tumults which at various times have happened in England, we shall find, that they did not proceed from the want of a government, but that government was itself the generating cause; instead of consolidating society, it divided it; it deprived it of its natural cohesion, and engendered discontents and disorders, which otherwise would not have existed. In those associations which men promiscuously form for the purpose of trade, or of any concern in which government is totally out of the question and in which they act merely on the principles of society, we see how naturally the various parties unite; and this shows, by comparison, that governments, so far from being always the cause or means of order, are often the destruction of it. The riots of 1780 had no other source than the remains of those prejudices which the government itself had encouraged. But with respect to England there are also other causes.

Excess and inequality of taxation, however disguised in the means, never fail to appear in their effect. As a great mass of the community are thrown thereby into poverty and discontent, they are constantly on the brink of commotion; and, deprived as they unfortunately are of the means of information, are easily heated to outrage. Whatever the apparent cause of any riots may be, the real one is always want of happiness. It shows that something is wrong in the system of government, that injures the felicity by which society is to be preserved.

But as fact is superior to reasoning, the instance of America presents itself to confirm these observations. If there is a country in the world, where concord, according to common calculation, would be least expected, it is America. Made up, as it is, of people from different nations,[1] accustomed to different forms and habits of government, speaking different languages, and more different in their modes of worship, it would appear that the union of such a people was impracticable; but by the simple operation of constructing government on the principles of society and the rights of man, every difficulty retires, and all the parts are brought into cordial unison. There, the poor are not oppressed, the rich are not privileged. Industry is not mortified by the splendid extravagance of a court rioting at its expense. Their taxes are few, be cause their government is just; and as there is nothing to render them wretched, there is nothing to engender riots and tumults.

A metaphysical man, like Mr. Burke, would have tortured his invention to discover how such a people could be governed. He would have supposed that some must be managed by fraud, others by force, and all by some contrivance; that genius must be hired to impose upon ignorance, and show and parade to fascinate the vulgar. Lost in the abundance of his researches, he would have resolved and re-resolved, and finally overlooked the plain and easy road that lay directly before him.

One of the great advantages of the American revolution has been that it led to a discovery of the principles and laid open the imposition of governments. All the revolutions till then had been worked within the atmosphere of a court, and never on the great floor of a nation. The parties were always of the

[1] That part of America which is generally called New England, including New Hampshire, Massachusetts, Rhode Island, and Connecticut, is peopled chiefly by English descendants. In the state of New York, about half are Dutch, the rest English, Scotch, and Irish. In New Jersey, a mixture of English and Dutch, with some Scotch and Irish. In Pennsylvania, about one third are English, another Germans, and the remainder Scotch and Irish, with some Swedes. The states to the southward have a greater proportion of English than the middle states, but in all of them there is a mixture; and besides those enumerated, there are a considerable number of French, and some few of all the European nations, lying on the coast. The most numerous religious denomination are the Presbyterians; but no one sect is established above another, and all men are equally citizens.

class of courtiers; and whatever was their rage for reformation, they carefully preserved the fraud of the profession.

In all cases they took care to represent government as a thing made up of mysteries which only themselves understood: and they hid from the understanding of the nation the only thing that was beneficial to know, namely, *that government is nothing more than a national association acting on the principles of society.*

Having thus endeavored to show that the social and civilized state of man is capable of performing within itself almost everything necessary to its protection and government, it will be proper, on the other hand, to take a review of the present old governments, and examine whether their principles and practice are correspondent thereto.

CHAPTER II. OF THE ORIGIN OF THE PRESENT OLD GOVERNMENTS

It is impossible that such governments as have hitherto existed in the world could have commenced by any other means than a total violation of every principle, sacred and moral. The obscurity in which the origin of all the present old governments is buried, implies the iniquity and disgrace with which they began. The origin of the present governments of America and France will ever be remembered, because it is honorable to record it; but with respect to the rest, even flattery has consigned them to the tomb of time, without an inscription.

It could have been no difficult thing in the early and solitary ages of the world, while the chief employment of men was that of attending flocks and herds, for a banditti of ruffians to overrun a country, and lay it under contribution. Their power being thus established, the chief of the band contrived to lose the name of robber in that of monarch; and hence the origin of monarchy and kings.

The origin of the government of England, so far as relates to what is called its line of monarchy, being one of the latest, is perhaps the best recorded. The hatred which the Norman invasion and tyranny begat must have been deeply rooted in the nation to have outlived the contrivance to obliterate it. Though not a courtier will talk of the curfew-bell, not a village in England has forgotten it.

Those bands of robbers having parcelled out the world and divided it into dominions, began, as is naturally the case, to quarrel with each other. What at first was obtained by violence was considered by others as lawful to be taken, and a second plunderer succeeded the first. They alternately invaded the dominions which each had assigned to himself, and the brutality with which they treated each other explains the original character of monarchy. It was ruffian torturing ruffian. The conqueror considered the conquered not as his prisoner, but his property. He led him in triumph rattling in chains, and doomed him, at pleasure, to slavery or death. As time obliterated the history of their beginning, their successors assumed new appearances to cut off the entail of their disgrace, but their principles and objects remained the same. What at first was plunder assumed the softer name of revenue; and the power originally usurped, they affected to inherit.

From such beginning of governments, what could be expected but a continual system of war and extortion? It has established itself into a trade. The vice is not peculiar to one more than to another, but is the common principle of all. There does not exist within such governments a stamina whereon to ingraft reformation; and the shortest and most effectual remedy is to begin anew.

What scenes of horror, what perfection of iniquity, present themselves in contemplating the character and reviewing the history of such governments! If we would delineate human nature with a baseness of heart and hypocrisy of countenance that reflection would shudder at and humanity disown, it is kings, courts, and cabinets, that must sit for the portrait. Man, as he is naturally, with all his faults about him, is not up to the character.

Can we possibly suppose that if government had originated in a right principle, and had not an interest in pursuing a wrong one, that the world could have been in the wretched and quarrelsome condition we have seen it? What inducement has the farmer, while following the plough, to lay aside his peaceful pursuits and go to war with the farmer of another country? Or what inducement has the manufacturer? What is dominion to them, or to any class of men in a nation? Does it add an acre to any man's estate, or raise its value? Are not conquest and defeat each of the same price, and taxes the never-failing consequence? Though this reasoning may be good to a nation, it is not so to a government. War is the faro-table of governments, and nations the dupes of the game.

If there is anything to wonder at in this miserable scene of governments, more than might be expected, it is the progress which the peaceful arts of agriculture, manufacture, and commerce have made, beneath such a long accumulating load of discouragement and oppression. It serves to show that instinct in animals does not act with stronger impulse than the principles of society and civilization operate in man. Under all discouragements, he pursues his object and yields to nothing but impossibilities.

CHAPTER III. OF THE OLD AND NEW SYSTEMS OF GOVERNMENT

Nothing can appear more contradictory than the principles on which the old governments began, and the condition to which society, civilization, and commerce, are capable of carrying mankind. Government on the old system is an assumption of power for the aggrandizement of itself; on the new, a delegation of power for the common benefit of society. The former supports itself by keeping up a system of war; the latter promotes a system of peace as the true means of enriching a nation. The one encourages national prejudices; the other promotes universal society as the means of universal commerce. The one measures its prosperity by the quantity of revenue it extorts; the other proves its excellence by the small quantity of taxes it requires.

Mr. Burke has talked of old and new whigs. If he can amuse himself with childish names and distinctions, I shall not interrupt his pleasure. It is not to him, but to the Abbé Sièyes, that I address this chapter. I am already engaged to the latter gentleman to discuss the subject of monarchical government; and as it naturally occurs in comparing the old and new systems, I make this the opportunity of presenting to him my observations. I shall occasionally take Mr. Burke in my way.

Though it might be proved that the system of government now called the *new* is the most ancient in principle of all that have existed, being founded on the original inherent rights of man: yet, as tyranny and the sword have suspended the exercise of those rights for many centuries past, it serves better the purpose of distinction to call it the *new* than to claim the right of calling it the old.

The first general distinction between those two systems is that the one now called the old is *hereditary*, either in whole or in part; and the new is entirely *representative*. It rejects all hereditary government:

1st, As being an imposition on mankind.

2d, As inadequate to the purposes for which government is necessary.

With respect to the first of these heads, it cannot be proved by what right hereditary government could begin; neither does there exist, within the compass of mortal power, a right to establish it. Man has no authority over posterity in matters of personal right; and therefore no man or body of men had, or can have, a right to set up hereditary government. Were even ourselves to come again into existence, instead of being succeeded by posterity, we have not now the right of taking from ourselves the rights which would then be ours. On what ground, then, do we pretend to take them from others?

All hereditary government is in its nature tyranny. A heritable crown, or a heritable throne, or by what other fanciful name such things may be called, have no other significant explanation than that mankind are heritable property.

To inherit a government is to inherit the people, as if they were flocks and herds.

With respect to the second head, that of being inadequate to the purposes for which government is necessary, we have only to consider what government essentially is and compare it with the circumstances to which hereditary succession is subject.

Government ought to be a thing always in full maturity. It ought to be so constructed as to be superior to all the accidents to which individual man is subject; and therefore, hereditary succession, by being *subject to them all*, is the most irregular and imperfect of all the systems of government.

We have heard the *rights of man* called a *leveling* system; but the only system to which the word *leveling* is truly applicable is the hereditary monarchical system. It is a system of *mental leveling*. It indiscriminately admits every species of character to the same authority. Vice and virtue, ignorance and wisdom, in short, every quality, good or bad, is put on the same level. Kings succeed each other, not as rationals, but as animals. Can we then be surprised at the abject state of the human mind in monarchical countries, when the government itself is formed on such an abject leveling system? It has no fixed character. Today it is one thing; and tomorrow it is something else. It changes with the temper of every succeeding individual, and is subject to all the varieties of each. It is government through the medium of passions and accidents. It appears under all the various characters of childhood, decrepitude, dotage, a thing at nurse, in leading strings, or on crutches. It reverses the wholesome order of nature. It occasionally puts children over men, and the conceits of non-age over wisdom and experience. In short, we cannot conceive a more ridiculous figure of government than hereditary succession, in all its cases, presents.

Could it be made a decree in nature, or an edict registered in heaven, and man could know it, that virtue and wisdom should invariably appertain to hereditary succession, the objections to it would be removed; but when we see that nature acts as if she disowned and sported with the hereditary system; that the mental characters of successors, in all countries, are below the average of human understanding; that one is a tyrant, another an idiot, a third insane, and some all three together, it is impossible to attach confidence to it, when reason in man has power to act.

It is not to the Abbé Sièyes that I need apply this reasoning; he has already saved me that trouble by giving his own opinion upon the case. "If it be asked," says he, "what is my opinion with respect to hereditary right, I answer, without hesitation that, in good theory, an hereditary transmission of any power or office can never accord with the laws of true representation. Hereditaryship is, in this sense, as much an attaint upon principle as an outrage upon society. But let us," continues he, "refer to the history of all elective monarchies and principalities; is there one in which the elective mode is not worse than the hereditary succession?"

As to debating on which is the worst of the two, is admitting both to be bad; and herein we are agreed. The preference which the abbé has given, is a condemnation of the thing he prefers. Such a mode of reasoning on such a subject is inadmissible, because it finally amounts to an accusation of providence, as if she had left to man no other choice with respect to government than between two evils, the best of which he admits to be "*an attaint upon principle, and an outrage upon society.*"

Passing over, for the present, all the evils and mischiefs which monarchy has occasioned in the world, nothing can more effectually prove its uselessness in a state of *civil government* than making it hereditary. Would we make any office hereditary that required wisdom and abilities to fill it? And where wisdom and abilities are not necessary, such an office, whatever it may be, is superfluous or insignificant.

Hereditary succession is a burlesque upon monarchy. It puts it in the most ridiculous light by presenting it as an office which any child or idiot may fill. It requires some talents to be a common mechanic; but to be a king requires only the animal figure of man—a sort of breathing automaton. This sort of superstition may last a few years more, but it cannot long resist the awakened reason and interest of man.

As to Mr. Burke, he is a stickler for monarchy, not altogether as a pensioner, if he is one, which I believe, but as a political man. He has taken up a contemptible opinion of mankind, who, in their turn, are taking up the same of him. He considers them as a herd of beings that must be governed by fraud, effigy, and show; and an idol would be as good a figure of monarchy with him, as a man. I will, however, do him the justice to say that, with respect to America, he has been very complimentary. He always contended, at least in my hearing, that the people of America were more enlightened than those of England, or of any country in Europe; and that therefore the imposition of show was not necessary in their governments.

Though the comparison between hereditary and elective monarchy, which the abbé had made, is unnecessary to the case, because the representative system rejects both; yet were I to make the comparison, I should decide contrary to what he has done.

The civil wars which have originated from contested hereditary claims are more numerous, and have been more dreadful, and of longer continuance than those which have been occasioned by election. All the civil wars in France arose from the hereditary system; they were either produced by hereditary claims, or by the imperfection of the hereditary form, which admits of regencies, or monarchy at nurse. With respect to England, its history is full of the same misfortunes. The contests for succession between the houses of York and Lancaster lasted a whole century; and others of a similar nature have renewed themselves since that period. Those of 1715 and 1745 were of the same kind. The succession-war for the crown of Spain embroiled almost half of Europe. The disturbances in Holland are generated from the hereditaryship of the stadt-holder. A government calling itself free, with an hereditary office, is like a thorn in the flesh that produces a fermentation which endeavors to discharge it.

But I might go further, and place also foreign wars, of whatever kind, to the same cause. It is by adding the evil of hereditary succession to that of monarchy that a permanent family interest is created, whose constant objects are dominion and revenue. Poland, though an elective monarchy, has had fewer wars than those which are hereditary; and it is the only government that has made a voluntary essay, though but a small one, to reform the condition of the country.

Having thus glanced at a few of the defects of the old, or hereditary systems of government, let us compare it with the new, or representative system.

The representative system takes society and civilization for its basis; nature, reason, and experience for its guide.

Experience, in all ages and in all countries, has demonstrated that it is impossible to control nature in her distribution of mental powers. She gives them as she pleases. Whatever is the rule by which she, apparently to us, scatters them among mankind, that rule remains a secret to man. It would be as ridiculous to attempt to fix the hereditaryship of human beauty, as of wisdom.

Whatever wisdom constituently is, it is like a seedless plant; it may be reared when it appears; but it cannot be voluntarily produced. There is always a sufficiency somewhere in the general mass of society for all purposes; but with respect to the parts of society, it is continually changing its place. It rises in one today, in another tomorrow and has most probably visited in rotation every family of the earth, and again withdrawn.

As this is the order of nature, the order of government must necessarily follow it, or government will, as we see it does, degenerate into ignorance. The hereditary system, therefore, is as repugnant to human wisdom as to human rights; and is as absurd as it is unjust.

As the republic of letters brings forward the best literary productions by giving to genius a fair and universal chance; so the representative system of government is calculated to produce the wisest laws by collecting wisdom where it can be found. I smile to myself when I contemplate the ridiculous insignificance into which literature and all the sciences would sink, were they made hereditary; and I carry the same idea into governments. An hereditary governor is as inconsistent as an hereditary author. I know not whether Homer or Euclid had sons; but I will venture an opinion that if they had, and had left their works unfinished, those sons could not have completed them.

Do we need a stronger evidence of the absurdity of hereditary government than is seen in descendants of those men, in any line of life, who once were famous? Is there scarcely an instance in which there is not a total reverse of the character? It appears as if the tide of mental faculties flowed as far as it could in certain channels, and then forsook its course and arose in others. How irrational then is the hereditary system which establishes channels of power in company with which wisdom refuses to flow! By continuing this absurdity, man is perpetually in contradiction with himself; he accepts, for a king, or a chief magistrate, or a legislator, a person whom he would not elect for a constable.

It appears to general observation that revolutions create genius and talents; but those events do no more than bring them forward. There exists in man a mass of sense lying in a dormant state, and which, unless something excites it to action, will descend with him, in that condition, to the grave. As it is to the advantage of society that the whole of its faculties should be employed, the construction of government ought to be such as to bring forward, by a quiet and regular operation, all that extent of capacity which never fails to appear in revolutions.

This cannot take place in the insipid state of hereditary government, not only because it prevents, but because it operates to benumb. When the mind of a nation is bowed down by any political superstition in its government, such as hereditary succession is, it loses a considerable portion of its powers on all other subjects and objects. Hereditary succession requires the same obedience to ignorance as to wisdom; and when once the mind can bring itself to pay this indiscriminate reverence, it descends below the stature of mental manhood. It is fit to be great only in little things. It acts a treachery upon itself, and suffocates the sensations that urge to detection.

Though the ancient governments present to us a miserable picture of the condition of man, there is one which above all others exempts itself from the general description. I mean the democracy of the Athenians. We see more to admire and less to condemn, in that great, extraordinary people, than in anything which history affords.

Mr. Burke is so little acquainted with constituent principles of government that he confounds democracy and representation together. Representation was a thing unknown in the ancient democracies. In those the mass of the people met and enacted laws (grammatically speaking) in the first person. Simple democracy was no other than the common hall of the ancients. It signifies the *form* as well as the public principle of the government. As these democracies increased in population, and the territory extended, the simple democratical form became unwieldly and impracticable; and as the system of representation was not known, the consequence was they either degenerated convulsively into monarchies or became absorbed into such as then existed. Had the system of representation been then understood, as it now is, there is no reason to believe that those forms of government now called monarchical or aristocratical would ever have taken place. It was the want of some method to consolidate the parts of society after it became too populous and too extensive for the simple democratical form, and also the lax and solitary condition of shepherds and herdsmen in other parts of the world, that afforded opportunities to those unnatural modes of government to begin.

As it is necessary to clear away the rubbish of errors into which the subject of government has been thrown, I shall proceed to remark on some others.

It has always been the political craft of courtiers and court governments to abuse something which they called republicanism; but what republicanism was, or is, they never attempt to explain. Let us examine a little into this case.

The only forms of government are the democratical, the aristocratical, the monarchical, and what is now called the representative.

What is called a *republic* is not any *particular form* of government. It is wholly characteristical of the purport, matter, or object for which government ought to be instituted, and on which it is to be employed, *res-publica*, the public affairs, or the public good; or, literally translated, the *public thing*. It is a word of a good original, referring to what ought to be the character and business of government; and in this sense it is naturally opposed to the word *monarchy*, which has a base original signification. It means arbitrary power in an individual person; in the exercise of which, *himself*, and not the *res-publica*, is the object.

Every government that does not act on the principle of a republic, or, in other words, that does not make the *res-publica* its whole and sole object, is not a good government. Republican government is no other than government established and conducted for the interest of the public, as well individually as collectively. It is not necessarily connected with any particular form, but it most naturally associates with the representative form, as being best calculated to secure the end for which a nation is at the expense of supporting it.

Various forms of government have affected to style themselves republics. Poland calls itself a republic, but is in fact an hereditary aristocracy, with what is called an elective monarchy. Holland calls itself a republic, which is chiefly aristocratical, with an hereditary stadtholdership. But the government of America, which is wholly on the system of representation, is the only real republic in character and practice that now exists. Its government has no other object than the public business of the nation, and therefore it is properly a republic; and the Americans have taken care that *this*, and no other, shall be the object of their government, by their rejecting everything hereditary and establishing government on the system of representation only.

Those who have said that a republic is not a *form* of government calculated for countries of great extent mistook, in the first place, the *business* of a government for a *form* of government; for the *res-publica* equally appertains to every extent of territory and population. And in the second place, if they meant anything with respect to *form*, it was the simple democratical form, such as was the mode of government in the ancient democracies, in which there was no representation. The case, therefore, is not that a republic cannot be extensive, but that it cannot be extensive on the simple democratic form; and the question naturally presents itself, *What is the best form of government for conducting the* RES-PUBLICA *or* PUBLIC BUSINESS *of a nation after it becomes too extensive and populous for the simple democratical form?*

It cannot be monarchy, because monarchy is subject to an objection of the same amount to which the democratical form was subject.

It is possible that an individual may lay down a system of principles on which government shall be constitutionally established to any extent of territory. This is no more than an operation of the mind, acting by its own powers. But the practice upon those principles, as applying to the various and numerous circumstances of a nation, its agriculture, manufactures, trade, commerce, &c. require a knowledge, of a different kind, and which can be had only from the various parts of society. It is an assemblage of practical knowledge which no one individual can possess; and therefore the monarchical form is as much limited, in useful practice, from the incompetency of knowledge, as was the democratical form from the multiplicity of population. The one degenerates, by extension, into confusion; the other, into ignorance and incapacity, of which all the great monarchies are an evidence. The monarchical form, therefore, could not be a substitute for the democratical, because it has equal inconveniences.

Much less could it when made hereditary. This is the most effectual of all forms to preclude knowledge. Neither could the high democratical mind have voluntarily yielded itself to be governed by children and idiots, and all the motley insignificance of character, which attends such a mere animal system, the disgrace and the reproach of reason and of man.

As to the aristocratical form, it has the same vices and defects with the monarchical, except that the chance of abilities is better from the proportion of numbers, but there is still no security for the right use and application of them.

Referring, then, to the original simple democracy, it affords the true data from which government on a large scale can begin. It is incapable of extension, not from its principle, but from the inconvenience of its form; and monarchy and aristocracy from their incapacity. Retaining, then, democracy as the ground, and rejecting the corrupt systems of monarchy and aristocracy, the representative system naturally presents itself; remedying at once the defects of the simple democracy as to form, and the incapacity of the other two with regard to knowledge.

Simple democracy was society governing itself without the use of secondary means. By ingrafting representation upon democracy, we arrive at a system of government capable of embracing and confederating all the various interests and every extent of territory and population; and that also with advantages as much superior to hereditary government as the republic of letters is to hereditary literature.

It is on this system that the American government is founded. It is representation ingrafted upon democracy. It has settled the form by a scale parallel in all cases to the extent of the principle. What Athens was in miniature, America will be in magnitude. The one was the wonder of the ancient world—the other is becoming the admiration and model of the present. It is the easiest of all the forms of government to be understood and the most eligible in practice; and excludes at once the ignorance and insecurity of the hereditary mode and the inconvenience of the simple democracy.

It is impossible to conceive a system of government capable of acting over such an extent of territory, and such a circle of interests, as is produced by the operation of representation. France, great and populous as it is, is but a spot in the capaciousness of the system. It adapts itself to all possible cases.

It is preferable to simple democracy even in small territories. Athens, by representation, would have surpassed her own democracy.

That which is called government, or rather that which we ought to conceive government to be, is no more than some common center in which all the parts of society unite. This cannot be established by any method so conducive to the various interests of the community as by the representative system. It concentrates the knowledge necessary to the interests of the parts and of the whole. It places government in a state of constant maturity. It is, as has been already observed, never young, never old. It is subject neither to nonage nor dotage. It is never in the cradle nor on crutches. It admits not of a separation between knowledge and power, and is superior, as government ought always to be, to all the accidents of individual man, and is therefore superior to what is called monarchy.

A nation is not a body, the figure of which is to be represented by the human body; but is like a body contained within a circle, having a common center in which every radius meets; and that center is formed by representation. To connect representation with what is called monarchy is eccentric government. Representation is of itself the delegated monarchy of a nation, and cannot debase itself by dividing it with another.

Mr. Burke has two or three times in his parliamentary speeches, and in his publications, made use of a jingle of words that convey no ideas. Speaking of government, he says, "It is better to have monarchy for its basis, and republicanism for its corrective, than republicanism for its basis, and monarchy for its corrective." If he means that it is better to correct folly with wisdom than wisdom with folly, I will no otherwise contend with him than to say it would be much better to reject the folly altogether.

But what is this thing which Mr. Burke calls monarchy? Will he explain it: all mankind can understand what representation is; and that it must necessarily include a variety of knowledge and talents. But what security is there for the same qualities on the part of monarchy? Or, when this monarchy is a child, where then is the wisdom? What does it know about government? Who then is the monarch? Or where is the monarchy? If it is to be performed by regency, it proves it to be a farce. A regency is a mock species of republic, and the whole of monarchy deserves no better appellation. It is a thing as various as imagination can paint. It has none of the stable character that government ought to possess. Every succession is a revolution, and every regency a counter-revolution. The whole of it is a scene of perpetual court cabal and intrigue, of which Mr. Burke is himself an instance.

Whether I have too little sense to see, or too much to be imposed upon; whether I have too much or too little pride, or of anything else, I leave out of the question; but certain it is that what is called monarchy always appears to me a silly, contemptible thing. I compare it to something kept behind a curtain, about which there is a great deal of bustle and fuss, and a wonderful air of seeming solemnity; but when, by any accident, the curtain happens to be open and the company see what it is, they burst into laughter.

In the representative system of government, nothing like this can happen. Like the nation itself, it possesses a perpetual stamina as well of body as of mind, and presents itself on the open theater of the world in a fair and manly manner. Whatever are its excellencies or its defects, they are visible to all. It exists not by fraud and mystery; it deals not in cant and sophistry; but inspires a language that, passing from heart to heart, is felt and understood.

We must shut our eyes against reason, we must basely degrade our understanding, not to see the folly of what is called monarchy. Nature is orderly in all her works; but this is a mode of government that counteracts nature. It turns the progress of the human faculties upside down. It subjects age to be governed by children, and wisdom by folly.

On the contrary, the representative system is always parallel with the order and immutable laws of nature, and meets the reason of man in every part. For example:

In the American federal government, more power is delegated to the President of the United States, than to any other individual member of congress. He cannot, therefore, be elected to this office under the age of thirty-five years. By this time the judgment of man becomes matured, and he has lived long enough to be acquainted with men and things, and the country with him. But on the monarchical plan (exclusive of the numerous chances there are against every man born into the world, of drawing a prize in the lottery of human faculties), the next in succession, whatever he may be, is put at the head of a nation, and of a government at the age of eighteen years. Does this appear like an act of wisdom? Is it consistent with the proper dignity and the manly character of a nation? Where is the propriety of calling such a lad the father of the people? In all other cases, a person is a minor until the age of twenty-one years. Before this period he is not trusted with the management of an acre of land, or with the heritable property of a flock of sheep, or a herd of swine; but wonderful to tell! he may at the age of eighteen years be trusted with a nation.

That monarchy is all a bubble, a mere court artifice to procure money, is evident (at least to me) in every character in which it can be viewed. It would be almost impossible, on the rational system of representative government, to make out a bill of expenses to such an enormous amount as this deception admits. Government is not of itself a very chargeable institution. The whole expense of the federal government of America, founded, as I have already said, on the system of representation, and extending over a country nearly ten times as large as England, is but six hundred thousand dollars, or one hundred and thirty thousand pounds sterling.

I presume that no man in his sober senses will compare the character of any of the kings of Europe, with that of General Washington. Yet, in France, and also in England, the expense of the civil list only, for the support of one man, is eight times greater than the whole expense of the federal government of America. To assign a reason for this appears almost impossible. The generality of people in America, especially the poor, are more able to pay taxes than the generality of people either in France or England.

But the case is that the representative system diffuses such a body of knowledge throughout the nation, on the subject of government, as to explode ignorance and preclude imposition. The craft of courts cannot be acted on that ground. There is no place for mystery; nowhere for it to begin. Those who are not in the representation know as much of the nature of business as those who are. An affectation of mysterious importance would there be scouted. Nations can have no secrets; and the secrets of courts, like those of individuals, are always their defects.

In the representative system, the reason for everything must publicly appear. Every man is a proprietor in government, and considers it a necessary part of his business to understand. It concerns his interest because it affects his property. He examines the cost, and compares it with the advantages; and above all, he does not adopt the slavish custom of following what in other governments are called *leaders*.

It can only be by blinding the understanding of man, and making him believe that government is some wonderful mysterious thing, that excessive revenues are obtained. Monarchy is well calculated to ensure this end. It is the popery of government; a thing kept up to amuse the ignorant, and quiet them into paying taxes.

The government of a free country, properly speaking, is not in the persons, but in the laws. The enacting of those requires no great expense; and when they are administered, the whole of civil government is performed—the rest is all court contrivance.

CHAPTER IV. OF CONSTITUTIONS

That men mean distinct and separate things when they talk of constitutions and of governments is evident; or why are those terms distinctly and separately used? A constitution is not the act of a government, but of a people constituting a government; and government without a constitution is power without a right.

All power exercised over a nation must have some beginning. It must be either delegated, or assumed. There are no other sources. All delegated power is trust, and all assumed power is usurpation. Time does not alter the nature and quality of either.

In viewing this subject, the case and circumstances of America present themselves as in the beginning of a world; and our inquiry into the origin of government is shortened by referring to the facts that have arisen in our day. We have no occasion to roam for information into the obscure field of antiquity, nor hazard ourselves upon conjecture. We are brought at once to the point of seeing government begin, as if we had lived in the beginning of time. The real volume, not of history, but of facts, is directly before us, unmutilated by contrivance or the errors of tradition.

I will here concisely state the commencement of the American constitutions; by which the difference between constitutions and governments will sufficiently appear.

It may not be improper to remind the reader that the United States of America consist of thirteen states, each of which established a government for itself, after the Declaration of Independence, of the fourth of July, 1776. Each state acted independently of the rest in forming its government; but the same general principle pervades the whole. When the several state governments were formed, they proceeded to form the federal government that acts over the whole in all matters which concern the interest of the whole, or which relate to the intercourse of the several states with each other, or with foreign nations. I will begin with giving an instance from one of the state governments (that of Pennsylvania) and then proceed to the federal government.

The state of Pennsylvania, though nearly of the same extent of territory as England, was then divided into twelve counties. Each of those counties had elected a committee at the commencement of the dispute with the English government; and as the city of Philadelphia, which also had its committee, was the most central for intelligence, it became the center of communication to the several county committees. When it became necessary to proceed to the formation of a government, the committee of Philadelphia proposed a conference of all the county committees to be held in that city, and which met the latter end of July, 1776.

Though these committees had been elected by the people, they were not elected expressly for the purpose, nor invested with the authority of forming a constitution: and as they could not, consistently with the American idea of rights, assume such a power, they could only confer upon the matter, and put it into a train of operation. The conferees, therefore, did no more than state the case and recommend to the several counties to elect six representatives for each county, to meet in convention at Philadelphia, with powers to form a constitution and propose it for public consideration.

This convention, of which Benjamin Franklin was president, having met and deliberated, and agreed upon a constitution, they next ordered it to be published, not as a thing established, but for the consideration of the whole people, their approbation or rejection, and then adjourned to a stated time. When the time of adjournment was expired, the convention reassembled; and as the general opinion of the people in approbation of it was then known, the constitution was signed, sealed, and proclaimed on the *authority of the people*, and the original instrument deposited as a public record. The convention then appointed a day for the general election of the representatives who were to compose the government, and the time it should commence; and having done this, they dissolved, and returned to their several homes and occupations.

In this constitution were laid down, first, a declaration of rights. Then followed the form which the government should have, and the powers it should possess—the authority of the courts of judicature and of juries—the manner in which elections should be conducted, and the proportion of representatives to the number of electors—the time which each succeeding assembly should continue, which was one year—the mode of levying and of accounting for the expenditure of public money —of appointing public officers, &c.

No article of this constitution could be altered or infringed at the discretion of the government that was to ensue. It was to that government a law. But as it would have been unwise to preclude the benefit of experience, and in order also to prevent the accumulation of errors, if any should be found, and to preserve a unison of government with the circumstances of the state at all times, the constitution provided that, at the expiration of every seven years, a convention should be elected; for the express purpose of revising the constitution, and making alterations, additions, or abolitions therein, if any such should be found necessary.

Here we see a regular process—a government issuing out of a constitution, formed by the people in their original character; and that constitution serving not only as an authority, but as a law of control to the government. It was the political bible of the state. Scarcely a family was without it. Every member of the government had a copy; and nothing was more common, when any debate arose on the principle of a bill, or on the extent of any species of authority, than for the members to take the printed constitution out of their pocket, and read the chapter with which such matter in debate was connected.

Having thus given an instance from one of the states, I will show the proceedings by which the federal constitution of the United States arose and was formed.

Congress, at its two first meetings, in September 1774 and May 1775, was nothing more than a deputation from the legislatures of the several provinces, afterwards states; and had no other authority than what arose from common consent and the necessity of its acting as a public body. In everything which related to the internal affairs of America, congress went no further than to issue recommendations, to the several provincial assemblies, who at discretion adopted them or not. Nothing on the part of congress was compulsive; yet, in this situation, it was more faithfully and affectionately obeyed, than was any government in Europe. This instance, like that of the national assembly of France, sufficiently shows that the strength of government does not consist in anything *within* itself, but in the attachment of a nation, and the interest which the people feel in supporting it. When this is lost, government is but a child in power; and though, like the old government of France, it may harass individuals for a while, it but facilitates its own fall.

After the Declaration of Independence, it became consistent with the principle on which representative government is founded that the authority of congress should be defined and established. Whether that authority should be more or less than congress then discretionarily exercised, was not then the question. It was merely the rectitude of the measure.

For this purpose the act, called the Act of Confederation (which was a sort of imperfect federal constitution), was proposed, and after long deliberation was concluded in the year 1781. It was not the act of congress, because it is repugnant to the principles of representative government that a body should give power to itself. Congress first informed the several states of the powers which it conceived were necessary to be invested in the union, to enable it to perform the duties and services required from it; and the states severally agreed with each other, and concentrated in congress those powers.

It may not be improper to observe that in both those instances (the one of Pennsylvania, and the other of the United States) there is no such thing as the idea of a compact between the people on one side, and the government on the other. The compact was that of the people with each other, to produce and constitute a government. To suppose that any government can be party in a compact with the whole people is to suppose it to have existence before it can have a right to exist. The only instance in which a compact can take place between the people and those who exercise the government is that the people shall pay them, while they choose to employ them.

Government is not a trade which any man or body of men has a right to set up and exercise for his own emolument, but is altogether a trust, in right of those by whom that trust is delegated, and by whom it is always resumable. It has of itself no rights; they are altogether duties.

Having thus given two instances of the original formation of a constitution, I will show the manner in which both have been changed since their first establishment.

The powers vested in the governments of the several states, by the state constitutions, were found, upon experience, to be too great; and those vested in the federal government, by the act of confederation, too little. The defect was not in the principle, but in the distribution of power.

Numerous publications, in pamphlets and in the newspapers, appeared on the propriety and necessity of new-modeling the federal government. After some time of public discussion, carried on through the channel of the press and in conversations, the state of Virginia, experiencing some inconvenience with respect to commerce, proposed holding a continental conference; in consequence of which a deputation from five or six of the state assemblies met at Annapolis in Maryland, in 1786. This meeting, not conceiving itself sufficiently authorized to go into the business of a reform, did no more than state their general opinions of the propriety of the measure and recommend that a convention of all the states should be held the year following.

This convention met at Philadelphia, in May 1787, of which General Washington was elected president. He was not at that time connected with any of the state governments or with congress. He delivered up his commission when the war ended, and since then had lived a private citizen.

The convention went deeply into all the subjects; and having, after a variety of debate and investigation, agreed among themselves upon the several parts of a federal constitution, the next question was the manner of giving it authority and practice.

For this purpose, they did not, like a cabal of courtiers, send for a Dutch stadtholder, or a German elector; but they referred the whole matter to the sense and interest of the country.

They first directed that the proposed constitution should be published. Second, that each state should elect a convention expressly for the purpose of taking it into consideration, and of ratifying or rejecting it; and that as soon as the approbation and ratification of any nine states should be given, that those states should proceed to the election of their proportion of members to the new federal government; and that the operation of it should then begin, and the former federal government cease.

The several states proceeded accordingly to elect their conventions; some of those conventions ratified the constitution by very large majorities, and two or three unanimously. In others there were much debate and division of opinion. In the Massachusetts convention, which met at Boston, the majority was not above nineteen or twenty, in about three hundred members; but such is the nature of representative government, that it quietly decides all matters by majority. After the debate in the Massachusetts convention was closed, and the vote taken, the objecting members rose and declared, "*That though they had argued and voted against it, because certain parts appeared to them in a different light to what they appeared to other members; yet as the vote had been decided in favor of the constitution as proposed, they should give it the same practical support as if they had voted for it.*"

As soon as nine states had concurred (and the rest followed in the order their conventions were elected), the old fabric of the federal government was taken down, and a new one erected, of which General Washington is president. In this place I cannot help remarking that the character and services of this gentleman are sufficient to put all those men called kings to shame. While they are receiving from the sweat and labors of mankind a prodigality of pay, to which neither their abilities nor their services can entitle them, he is rendering every service in his power, and refusing every pecuniary reward. He accepted no pay as commander-in-chief; he accepts none as president of the United States.

After the new federal constitution was established, the state of Pennsylvania, conceiving that some parts of its own constitution required to be altered, elected a convention for that purpose. The proposed alterations were published, and the people concurring therein, they were established.

In forming those constitutions, or in altering them, little or no inconvenience took place. The ordinary course of things was not interrupted, and the advantages have been much. It is always the interest of a far greater number of people in a nation to have things right than to let them remain wrong; and when public matters are open to debate, and the public judgment free, it will not decide wrong unless it decides too hastily.

In the two instances of changing the constitutions, the government then in being were not actors either way. Government has no right to make itself a party in any debate respecting the principles or modes of forming or of changing constitutions. It is not for the benefit of those who exercise the powers of government, that constitutions, and the governments issuing from them, are established. In all those matters, the right of judging and acting are in those who pay, and not in those who receive.

A constitution is the property of a nation, and not of those who exercise the government. All the constitutions of America are declared to be established on the authority of the people. In France, the word nation is used instead of the people; but in both cases, a constitution is a thing antecedent to the government, and always distinct therefrom.

In England, it is not difficult to perceive that everything has a constitution, except the nation. Every society and association that is established first agreed upon a number of original articles, digested into form, which are its constitution. It then appointed its officers, whose powers and authorities are described in that constitution, and the government of that society then commenced. Those officers, by whatever name they are called, have no authority to add to, alter, or abridge the original articles. It is only to the constituting power that this right belongs.

From the want of understanding the difference between a constitution and a government, Dr. Johnson, and all writers of his description, have always bewildered themselves. They could not but perceive that there must necessarily be a *controlling* power existing somewhere, and they placed this power in the discretion of the persons exercising the government, instead of placing it in a constitution formed by the nation. When it is in a constitution, it has the nation for its support, and the natural and the political controlling powers are together. The laws which are enacted by governments control men only as individuals, but the nation, through its constitution, controls the whole government, and has a natural ability so to do. The final controlling power, therefore, and the original constituting power are one and the same power.

Dr. Johnson could not have advanced such a position in any country where there was a constitution; and he is himself an evidence that no such thing as a constitution exists in England. But it may be put as a question, not improper to be investigated, that if a constitution does not exist, how came the idea of its existence so generally established?

In order to decide this question, it is necessary to consider a constitution in both its cases: 1st, as creating a government and giving it powers; 2d, as regulating and restraining the powers so given.

If we begin with William of Normandy, we find that the government of England was originally a tyranny, founded on an invasion and conquest of the country. This being admitted, it will then appear that the exertion of the nation, at different periods, to abate that tyranny and render it less intolerable, has been credited for a constitution.

Magna Charta, as it was called (it is now like an almanac of the same date), was no more than compelling the government to renounce a part of its assumptions. It did not create and give powers to government in the manner a constitution does; but was, as far as it went, of the nature of a re-conquest, and not of a constitution; for, could the nation have totally expelled the usurpation, as France has done its despotism, it would then have had a constitution to form.

The history of the Edwards and the Henrys, and up to the commencement of the Stuarts, exhibits as many instances of tyranny as could be acted within the limits to which the nation had restricted it. The Stuarts endeavored to pass those limits, and their fate is well-known. In all those instances we see nothing of a constitution, but only of restrictions on assumed power.

After this, another William, descended from the same stock, and claiming from the same origin, gained possession; and of the two evils, James and William, the nation preferred what it thought the least; since, from the circumstances, it must take one. The act, called the Bill of Rights, comes here into view. What is it but a bargain which the parts of the government made with each other to divide power, profit, and privileges? You shall have so much, and I will have the rest; and with respect to the nation, it said, for *your share*, YOU *shall have the right of petitioning*. This being the case, the bill of rights is more properly a bill of wrongs and of insult. As to what is called the convention-parliament, it was a thing that made itself, and then made the authority by which it acted. A few persons got together and called themselves by that name. Several of them had never been elected, and none of them for the purpose.

From the time of William, a species of government arose, issuing out of this coalition bill of rights; and more so, since the corruption introduced at the Hanover succession by the agency of Walpole: that can be described by no other name than a despotic legislation. Though the parts may embarrass each other, the whole has no bounds; and the only right it acknowledges out of itself is the right of petitioning. Where then is the constitution that either gives or restrains power?

It is not because a part of the government is elective that makes it less a despotism, if the persons so elected possess afterwards, as a parliament, unlimited powers. Election, in this case, becomes separated from representation, and the candidates are candidates for despotism.

I cannot believe that any nation, reasoning on its own rights, would have thought of calling those things a *constitution*, if the cry of constitution had not been set up by the government. It has got into circulation, like the words *bore* and *quiz*, by being chalked up in speeches of parliament, as those words were on window shutters and doorposts; but whatever the constitution may be in other respects, it has undoubtedly been *the most productive machine for taxation that was ever invented.* The taxes in France, under the new constitution, are not quite thirteen shillings per head,[1] and the taxes in England, under what is called its present constitution, are forty-eight shillings and sixpence per head, men, women, and children, amounting to nearly seventeen millions sterling, besides the expense of collection, which is upwards of a million more.

In a country like England, where the whole of the civil government is executed by the people of every town and county by means of parish officers, magistrates, quarterly sessions, juries, and assize, without any trouble to what is called government, or any other expense to the revenue than the salary of the judges, it is astonishing how such a mass of taxes can be employed. Not even the internal defense of the country is paid out of the revenue. On all occasions, whether real or contrived, recourse is continually had to new loans and to new taxes. No wonder, then, that a machine of government so advantageous to the advocates of a court should be so triumphantly extolled! No wonder that St. James's or St. Stephen's should echo with the continual cry of constitution! No wonder that the French revolution should be reprobated, and the *res-publica* treated with reproach! The *red book* of England, like the red book of France, will explain the reason.[2]

I will now, by way of relaxation, turn a thought or two to Mr. Burke. I ask his pardon for neglecting him so long.

[1] The whole amount of the assessed taxes of France, for the present year, is three hundred millions of francs, which is twelve millions and a half sterling; and the incidental taxes are estimated at three millions, making in the whole fifteen millions and an half; which among twenty-four millions of people, is not quite thirty shillings per head. France has lessened her taxes since the revolution, nearly nine millions sterling annually. Before the revolution the city of Paris paid a duty of upwards of thirty per cent on all articles brought into the city. This tax was collected at the city gates. It was taken off on the first of last May, and the gates taken down. [Paine's note.]

[2] What was called the *livre rouge*, or the red book, in France, was not exactly similar to the court calendar in England; but it sufficiently showed how a great part of the taxes were lavished.

"America," says he (in his speech on the Canada constitution bill), "never dreamed of such absurd doctrine as the Rights of Man."

Mr. Burke is such a bold presumer, and advances his assertions and premises with such a deficiency of judgment, that, without troubling ourselves about principles of philosophy or politics, the mere logical conclusions they produce are ridiculous. For instance:

If governments, as Mr. Burke asserts, are not founded on the rights of *man*, and are founded on *any rights* at all, they consequently must be founded on the rights of *something* that is *not man*. What, then, is that something?

Generally speaking, we know of no other creatures that inhabit the earth than man and beast; and in all cases where only two things offer themselves and one must be admitted, a negation proved on any one amounts to an affirmative on the other; and therefore, Mr. Burke, by proving against the rights of *man*, proves in behalf of the *beast;* and consequently, proves that government is a beast: and as difficult things sometimes explain each other, we now see the origin of keeping wild beasts in the Tower; for they certainly can be of no other use than to show the origin of the government. They are in the place of a constitution. O! John Bull, what honors thou hast lost by not being a wild beast. Thou mightest, on Mr. Burke's system, have been in the Tower for life.

If Mr. Burke's arguments have not weight enough to keep one serious, the fault is less mine than his; and as I am willing to make an apology to the reader for the liberty I have taken, I hope Mr. Burke will also make his for giving the cause.

Having thus paid Mr. Burke the compliment of remembering him, I return to the subject.

From the want of a constitution in England to restrain and regulate the wild impulse of power, many of the laws are irrational and tyrannical, and the administration of them vague and problematical.

The attention of the government of England (for I rather choose to call it by this name, than the English government) appears, since its political connection with Germany, to have been so completely engrossed and absorbed by foreign affairs, and the means of raising taxes, that it seems to exist for no other purposes. Domestic concerns are neglected; and, with respect to regular law, there is scarcely such a thing.

Almost every case must now be determined by some precedent, be that precedent good or bad, or whether it properly applies or not; and the practice is become so general, as to suggest a suspicion, that it proceeds from a deeper policy than at first sight appears.

Since the revolution of America, and more so since that of France, this preaching up the doctrine of precedents, drawn from times and circumstances antecedent to those events, has been the studied practice of the English government. The generality of those precedents are founded on principles and opinions the reverse of what they ought to be; and the greater distance of time they are drawn from, the more they are to be suspected. But by associating those precedents with a superstitious reverence for ancient things, as monks show relics and call them holy, the generality of mankind are deceived into the design. Governments now act as if they were afraid to awaken a single reflection in man. They are softly leading him to the sepulcher of precedents to deaden his faculties and call his attention from the scene of revolutions. They feel that he is arriving at knowledge faster than they wish, and their policy of precedents is the barometer of their fears. This political popery, like the ecclesiastical popery of old, has had its day and is hastening to its exit. The ragged relic and the antiquated precedent, the monk and the monarch, will moulder together.

Government by precedent, without any regard to the principle of the precedent, is one of the vilest systems that can be set up. In numerous instances the precedent ought to operate as a warning and not as an example, and requires to be shunned instead of imitated; but instead of this, precedents are taken in the lump and put at once for constitution and for law.

Either the doctrine of precedent is policy to keep a man in a state of ignorance, or it is a practical confession that wisdom degenerates in governments as governments increase in age, and can only hobble along by the stilts and crutches of precedents. How is it that the same persons who would proudly be thought wiser than their predecessors, appear at the same time only as the ghosts of departed wisdom? How strangely is antiquity treated! To answer some purposes it is spoken of as the times of darkness and ignorance, and to answer others it is put for the light of the world.

If the doctrine of precedents is to be followed, the expenses of government need not continue the same. Why pay men extravagantly who have but little to do? If everything that can happen is already in precedent, legislation is at an end, and precedent, like a dictionary, determines every case. Either, therefore, government has arrived at its dotage and requires to be renovated, or all the occasions for exercising its wisdom have occurred.

We now see all over Europe, and particularly in England, the curious phenomenon of a nation looking one way, and a government the other; the one forward, and the other backward. If governments are to go on by precedent while nations go on by improvement they must at last come to a final separation, and the sooner and the more civilly they determine this point, the better it will be for them.[1]

Having thus spoken of constitutions generally as things distinct from actual governments, let us proceed to consider the parts of which a constitution is composed.

[1] In England, the improvements in agriculture, useful arts, manufactures, and commerce have been made in opposition to the genius of its government, which is that of following precedents. It is from the enterprise and industry of the individuals and their numerous associations, in which, tritely speaking, government is neither pillow nor bolster, that these improvements have proceeded. No man thought about the government, or who was in, or who was out, when he was planning or executing those things: and all he had to hope, with respect to government, was that it would let him alone. Three or four very silly ministerial newspapers are continually offending against the spirit of national improvement, by ascribing it to a minister. They may with as much truth ascribe this book to a minister.

Opinions differ more on this subject than with respect to the whole. That a nation ought to have a constitution as a rule for the conduct of its government, is a simple question in which all men, not directly courtiers, will agree. It is only on the component parts that questions and opinions multiply.

But this difficulty, like every other, will diminish when put into a train of being rightly understood.

The first thing is that a nation has a right to establish a constitution.

Whether it exercises this right in the most judicious manner at first is quite another case. It exercises it agreeably to the judgment it possesses; and by continuing to do so, all errors will at last be exploded.

When this right is established in a nation, there is no fear that it will be employed to its own injury. A nation can have no interest in being wrong.

Though all the constitutions of America are on one general principle, yet no two of them are exactly alike in their component parts, or in the distribution of the powers which they give to the actual governments. Some are more and others less complex.

In forming a constitution it is first necessary to consider what are the ends for which government is necessary: secondly, what are the best means, and the least expensive, for accomplishing those ends.

Government is nothing more than a national association; and the object of this association is the good of all, as well individually as collectively. Every man wishes to pursue his occupation, and to enjoy the fruits of his labors and the produce of his property in peace and safety, and with the least possible expense. When these things are accomplished, all the objects for which government ought to be established are answered.

It has been customary to consider government under three distinct general heads. The legislative, the executive, and the judicial.

But if we permit our judgment to act unincumbered by the habit of multiplied terms, we can perceive no more than two divisions of power of which civil government is composed, namely, that of legislating or enacting laws, and that of executing or administering them. Everything, therefore, appertaining to civil government, classes itself under one or other of these two divisions.

So far as regards the execution of the laws, that which is called the judicial power is strictly and properly the executive power of every country. It is that power to which every individual has an appeal, and which causes the laws to be executed; neither have we any other clear idea with respect to the official execution of the laws. In England, and also in America and France, this power begins with the magistrate and proceeds up through all the courts of judicature.

I leave to courtiers to explain what is meant by calling monarchy the executive power. It is merely a name in which acts of government are done; and any other, or none at all, would answer the same purpose. Laws have neither more nor less authority on this account. It must be from the justness of their principles, and the interest which a nation feels therein, that they derive support; if they require any other than this, it is a sign that something in the system of government is imperfect. Laws difficult to be executed cannot be generally good.

With respect to the organization of the *legislative power*, different modes have been adopted in different countries. In America it is generally composed of two houses. In France it consists but of one, but in both countries it is wholly by representation.

The case is that mankind (from the long tyranny of assumed power) have had so few opportunities of making the necessary trials on modes and principles of government, in order to discover the best, *that government is but now beginning to be known*, and experience is yet wanting to determine many particulars.

The objections against two houses are, first, that there is an inconsistency in any part of a whole legislature coming to a final determination by vote on any matter, whilst *that matter* with respect to *that whole* is yet only in a train of deliberation, and consequently open to new illustrations.

2d, That by taking the vote on each, as a separate body, it always admits of the possibility, and is often the case in practice, that the minority governs the majority, and that, in some instances, to a great degree of inconsistency.

3d, That two houses arbitrarily checking or controlling each other, is inconsistent; because it cannot be proved, on the principles of just representation, that either should be wiser or better than the other. They may check in the wrong as well as in the right; and therefore to give the power where we cannot give the wisdom to use it, nor be assured of its being rightly used, renders the hazard at least equal to the precaution.[1]

The objection against a single house is that it is always in a condition of committing itself too soon. But it should at the same time be remembered that when there is a constitution

[1]With respect to the two houses, of which the English parliament is composed, they appear to be effectually influenced into one, and, as a legislature, to have no temper of its own. The minister, whoever he at any time may be, touches it as with an opium wand and it sleeps obedience.

But if we look at the distinct abilities of the two houses, the difference will appear so great as to show the inconsistency of placing power where there can be no certainty of the judgment to use it. Wretched as the state of representation is in England, it is manhood compared with what is called the house of lords; and so little is this nicknamed house regarded that the people scarcely inquire at any time what it is doing. It appears also to be most under influence and the furthest removed from the general interest of the nation. In the debate on engaging in the Russian and Turkish war, the majority in the house of peers in favor of it was upwards of ninety, when in the other house, which is more than double its numbers, the majority was sixty-three.

The proceedings on Mr. Fox's bill, respecting the rights of juries, merits also to be noticed. The persons called the peers were not the objects of that bill. They are already in possession of more privileges than that bill gave to others. They are their own jury, and if any one of that house were prosecuted for a libel, he would not suffer, even upon conviction, for the first offense. Such inequality in laws ought not to exist in any country. The French constitution says that *the law is the same to every individual, whether to protect or to punish. All are equal in its sight.*

which defines the power and establishes the principles within which a legislature shall act, there is already a more effectual check provided, and more powerfully operating, than any other check can be. For example,

Were a bill to be brought into any of the American legislatures, similar to that which was passed into an act by the English parliament, at the commencement of the reign of George I, to extend the duration of the assemblies to a longer period than they now sit, the check is in the constitution, which in effect says *thus far shalt thou go and no further.*

But in order to remove the objection against a single house (that of acting with too quick an impulse) and at the same time to avoid the inconsistencies, in some cases absurdities, arising from the two houses, the following method has been proposed as an improvement on both.

1st, To have but one representation.

2d, To divide that representation, by lot, into two or three parts.

3d, That every proposed bill shall first be debated in those parts, by succession, that they may become hearers of each other, but without taking any vote. After which the whole representation to assemble for a general debate and determination by vote.

To this proposed improvement has been added another for the purpose of keeping the representation in a state of constant renovation; which is, that one third of the representation of each county shall go out at the expiration of one year, and the number be replaced by new elections. Another third at the expiration of the second year, replaced in like manner, and every third year to be a general election.[1]

But in whatever manner the separate parts of a constitution may be arranged, there is one general principle that distin-

[1] As to the state of representation in England, it is too absurd to be reasoned upon. Almost all the represented parts are decreasing in population and the unrepresented parts are increasing. A general convention of the nation is necessary to take the whole state of its government into consideration.

guishes freedom from slavery, which is that all *hereditary government over a people is to them a species of slavery and representative government is freedom.*

Considering government in the only light in which it should be considered, that of a NATIONAL ASSOCIATION, it ought to be so constructed as not to be disordered by any accident happening among the parts; and therefore no extraordinary power, capable of producing such an effect, should be lodged in the hands of any individual. The death, sickness, absence, or defection, of any one individual in a government ought to be a matter of no more consequence, with respect to the nation, than if the same circumstance had taken place in a member of the English parliament, or the French national assembly.

Scarcely anything presents a more degrading character of national greatness than its being thrown into confusion by anything happening to or acted by an individual; and the ridiculousness of the scene is often increased by the natural insignificance of the person by whom it is occasioned. Were a government so constructed that it could not go on unless a goose or a gander were present in the senate, the difficulties would be just as great and as real on the flight or sickness of the goose or the gander, as if they were called a king. We laugh at individuals for the silly difficulties they make to themselves, without perceiving that the greatest of all ridiculous things are acted in governments.[1]

---

[1]It is related that in the canton of Berne, in Switzerland, it had been customary from time immemorial to keep a bear at the public expense, and the people had been taught to believe that if they had not a bear they should all be undone. It happened some years ago that the bear then in being was taken sick and died too suddenly to have his place immediately supplied with another. During the interregnum the people discovered that the corn grew and the vintage flourished, and the sun and moon continued to rise and set, and everything went on the same as before, and, taking courage from these circumstances, they resolved not to keep any more bears: for, said they, "a bear is a very voracious, expensive animal, and we were obliged to pull out his claws, lest he should hurt the citizens." The story of the bear of Berne was related in some of the French newspapers at the time of the flight of Louis XVI, and the applica-

All the constitutions of America are on a plan that excludes the childish embarrassments which occur in monarchical countries. No suspension of government can there take place for a moment from any circumstance whatever. The system of representation provides for everything, and is the only system in which nations and governments can always appear in their proper character.

As extraordinary power ought not be lodged in the hands of any individual, so ought there to be no appropriations of public money to any person beyond what his services in a state may be worth. It signifies not whether a man be called a president, a king, an emperor, a senator, or by any other name which propriety or folly may devise or arrogance assume; it is only a certain service he can perform in the state; and the service of any such individual in the routine of office, whether such office be called monarchical, presidential, senatorial, or by another name or title, can never exceed the value of ten thousand pounds a year. All the great services that are done in the world are performed by volunteer characters who accept no pay for them; but the routine of office is always regulated to such a general standard of abilities as to be within the compass of numbers in every country to perform, and therefore cannot merit very extraordinary recompense. *Government*, says Swift, *is a plain thing, and fitted to the capacity of many heads.*

It is inhuman to talk of a million sterling a year, paid out of the public taxes of any country, for the support of any individual, whilst thousands who are forced to contribute thereto are pining with want and struggling with misery. Government does not consist in a contrast between prisons and palaces, between poverty and pomp; it is not instituted to rob the needy of his mite and increase the wretchedness of the wretched. But of this part of the subject I shall speak hereafter, and confine myself at present to political observations.

When extraordinary power and extraordinary pay are allotted

---

tion of it to monarchy could not be mistaken in France; but it seems that the aristocracy of Berne applied it to themselves, and have since prohibited the reading of French newspapers.

to any individual in a government, he becomes the center round which every kind of corruption generates and forms. Give to any man a million a year, and add thereto the power of creating and disposing of places at the expense of a country, and the liberties of that country are no longer secure. What is called the splendor of a throne is no other than the corruption of the state. It is made up of a band of parasites living in luxurious indolence out of the public taxes.

When once such a vicious system is established, it becomes the guard and protection of all inferior abuses. The man who is in the receipt of a million a year is the last person to promote a spirit of reform, lest, in the event, it should reach to himself. It is always his interest to defend inferior abuses as so many outworks to protect the citadel; and in this species of political fortification, all the parts have such a common dependence that it is never to be expected they will attack each other.[1]

Monarchy would not have continued so many ages in the

[1] It is scarcely possible to touch on any subject that will not suggest an allusion to some corruption in governments. The simile of *"fortifications"* unfortunately involves with it a circumstance which is directly in point with the matter above alluded to.

Among the numerous instances of abuse which have been acted or protected by governments, ancient or modern, there is not a greater than that of quartering a man and his heirs upon the public, to be maintained at its expense.

Humanity dictates a provision for the poor—but by what right, moral or political, does any government assume to say that the person called the duke of Richmond shall be maintained by the public? Yet, if common report is true, not a beggar in London can purchase his wretched pittance of coal without paying towards the civil list of the duke of Richmond. Were the whole produce of this imposition but a shilling a year, the iniquitous principle would be still the same —but when it amounts, as it is said to do, to not less than twenty thousand pounds per ann. the enormity is too serious to be permitted to remain.—This is one of the effects of monarchy and aristocracy.

In stating this case, I am led by no personal dislike. Though I think it mean in any man to live upon the public, the vice originates in the government; and so general is it become that whether the parties are in the ministry or in the opposition it makes no difference; they are sure of the guarantee of each other.

world had it not been for the abuses it protects. It is the master-fraud which shelters all others. By admitting a participation of the spoil, it makes itself friends; and when it ceases to do this, it will cease to be the idol of courtiers.

As the principle on which constitutions are now formed rejects all hereditary pretensions to government, it also rejects all that catalogue of assumptions known by the name of prerogatives.

If there is any government where prerogatives might with apparent safety be intrusted to any individual, it is in the federal government of America. The president of the United States of America is elected only for four years. He is not only responsible in the general sense of the word, but a particular mode is laid down in the constitution for trying him. He cannot be elected under thirty-five years of age; and he must be a native of the country.

In a comparison of these cases with the government of England, the difference when applied to the latter amounts to an absurdity. In England, the person who exercises the prerogative is often a foreigner; always half a foreigner, and always married to a foreigner. He is never in full natural or political connection with the country, is not responsible for anything, and becomes of age at eighteen years; yet such a person is permitted to form foreign alliances without even the knowledge of the nation; and to make war and peace without its consent.

But this is not all. Though such a person cannot dispose of the government, in the manner of a testator, he dictates the marriage connections which, in effect, accomplishes a great part of the same end. He cannot directly bequeath half the government to Prussia, but he can form a marriage partnership that will produce the same effect. Under such circumstances, it is happy for England that she is not situated on the continent, or she might, like Holland, fall under the dictatorship of Prussia. Holland, by marriage, is as effectually governed by Prussia as if the old tyranny of bequeathing the government had been the means.

The presidency in America (or, as it is sometimes called, the executive) is the only office from which a foreigner is excluded; and in England it is the only one to which he is admitted. A foreigner cannot be a member of parliament, but he may be what is called a king. If there is any reason for excluding foreigners, it ought to be from those offices where most mischief can be acted, and where, by uniting every bias of interest and attachment, the trust is best secured.

But as nations proceed in the great business of forming constitutions they will examine with more precision into the nature and business of that department which is called the executive. What the legislative and judicial departments are, everyone can see; but with respect to what, in Europe, is called the executive, as distinct from those two, it is either a political superfluity or a chaos of unknown things.

Some kind of official department, to which reports shall be made from different parts of the nation, or from abroad, to be laid before the national representatives, is all that is necessary; but there is no consistency in calling this the executive; neither can it be considered in any other light than as inferior to the legislature. The sovereign authority in any country is the power of making laws, and everything else is an official department.

Next to the arrangement of the principles and the organization of the several parts of a constitution is the provision to be made for the support of the persons to whom the nation shall confide the administration of the constitutional powers.

A nation can have no right to the time and services of any person at his own expense, whom it may choose to employ or intrust in any department whatever; neither can any reason be given for making provision for the support of any one part of the government and not for the other.

But, admitting that the honor of being intrusted with any part of a government is to be considered a sufficient reward, it ought to be so to every person alike. If the members of the legislature of any country are to serve at their own expense, that which is called the executive, whether monarchical or by any other name, ought to serve in like manner. It is inconsistent to pay the one, and accept the service of the other gratis.

In America every department in the government is decently provided for; but no one is extravagantly paid. Every member of congress and of the state assemblies is allowed a sufficiency for his expenses. Whereas in England, a most prodigal provision is made for the support of one part of the government and none for the other; the consequence of which is that the one is furnished with the means of corruption, and the other is put into the condition of being corrupted. Less than a fourth part of such expense, applied as it is in America, would remedy a great part of the corruption.

Another reform in the American constitutions is the exploding all oaths of personality. The oath of allegiance is to the nation only. The putting any individual as a figure for a nation is improper. The happiness of a nation is the first object, and therefore the intention of an oath of allegiance ought not to be obscured by being figuratively taken to, or in the name of, any person. The oath, called the civic oath, in France, *viz.* the "*nation, the law, and the king,*" is improper. If taken at all it ought to be, as in America, to the nation only. The law may or may not be good; but, in this place, it can have no other meaning than as being conducive to the happiness of the nation, and therefore is included in it. The remainder of the oath is improper, on the ground that all personal oaths ought to be abolished. They are the remains of tyranny on one part, and slavery on the other; and the name of the Creator ought not to be introduced to witness the degradation of his creation; or if taken, as is already mentioned, as figurative of the nation, it is in this place redundant. But whatever apology may be made for oaths at the first establishment of a government, they ought not to be permitted afterwards. If a government requires the support of oaths, it is a sign that it is not worth supporting, and ought not to be supported. Make government what it ought to be, and it will support itself.

To conclude this part of the subject. One of the greatest

improvements that has been made for the perpetual security and progress of constitutional liberty is the provision which the new constitutions make for occasionally revising, altering, and amending them.

The principle upon which Mr. Burke formed his political creed, that "*of binding and controlling posterity to the end of time, and renouncing and abdicating the rights of all posterity forever,*" is now become too detestable to be made a subject of debate; and, therefore, I pass it over with no other notice than exposing it.

Government is but now beginning to be known. Hitherto it has been the mere exercise of power which forbad all effectual inquiry into rights, and grounded itself wholly on possession. While the enemy of liberty was its judge, the progress of its principles must have been small indeed.

The constitutions of America, and also that of France, have either fixed a period for their revision or laid down the mode by which improvements shall be made. It is perhaps impossible to establish anything that combines principles with opinions and practice, which the progress of circumstances, through a length of years, will not in some measure derange or render inconsistent; and, therefore, to prevent inconveniences accumulating, till they discourage reformations or provoke revolutions, it is best to regulate them as they occur. The rights of man are the rights of all generations of men, and cannot be monopolized by any. That which is worth following, will be followed for the sake of its worth; and it is in this that its security lies, and not in any conditions with which it may be incumbered. When a man leaves property to his heirs, he does not connect it with an obligation that they shall accept it. Why then should we do otherwise with respect to constitutions?

The best constitution that could now be devised, consistent with the condition of the present moment, may be far short of that excellence which a few years may afford. There is a morning of reason rising upon man, on the subject of government, that has not appeared before. As the barbarism of the present old governments expires, the moral condition of nations with respect to each other will be changed. Man will not be brought up with the savage idea of considering his species as enemies because the accident of birth gave the individuals existence in countries distinguished by different names; and as constitutions have always some relation to external as well as to domestic circumstances, the means of benefiting by every change, foreign or domestic, should be a part of every constitution.

We already see an alteration in the national disposition of England and France towards each other, which, when we look back only a few years, is itself a revolution. Who could have foreseen, or who would have believed, that a French national assembly would ever have been a popular toast in England, or that a friendly alliance of the two nations should become the wish of either? It shows that man, were he not corrupted by governments, is naturally the friend of man, and that human nature is not of itself vicious. That spirit of jealousy and ferocity, which the governments of the two countries inspired and which they rendered subservient to the purpose of taxation, is now yielding to the dictates of reason, interest, and humanity. The trade of courts is beginning to be understood, and the affectation of mystery, with all the artificial sorcery by which they imposed upon mankind, is on the decline. It has received its death wound; and though it may linger, it will expire.

Government ought to be as much open to improvement as anything which appertains to man, instead of which it has been monopolized from age to age by the most ignorant and vicious of the human race. Need we any other proof of their wretched management than the excess of debts and taxes with which every nation groans, and the quarrels into which they have precipitated the world?

Just emerging from such a barbarous condition, it is too soon to determine to what extent of improvement government may yet be carried. For what we can foresee, all Europe may form but one great republic, and man be free of the whole.

CHAPTER V. WAYS AND MEANS OF IMPROVING THE CONDITION OF EUROPE: INTERSPERSED WITH MISCELLANEOUS OBSERVATIONS

In contemplating a subject that embraces with equatorial magnitude the whole region of humanity, it is impossible to confine the pursuit in any one single direction. It takes ground on every character and condition that appertains to man, and blends the individual, the nation, and the world.

From a small spark, kindled in America, a flame has arisen not to be extinguished. Without consuming, like the *ultima ratio regum*, it winds its progress from nation to nation, and conquers by a silent operation. Man finds himself changed, he scarcely perceives how. He acquires a knowledge of his rights by attending justly to his interest, and discovers in the event that the strength and powers of despotism consist wholly in the fear of resisting it, and that, in order *"to be free, it is sufficient that he wills it."*

Having in all the preceding parts of this work endeavored to establish a system of principles as a basis on which governments ought to be erected, I shall proceed in this, to the ways and means of rendering them into practice. But in order to introduce this part of the subject with more propriety and stronger effect, some preliminary observations, deducible from or connected with those principles, are necessary.

Whatever the form or constitution of government may be, it ought to have no other object than the general happiness. When, instead of this, it operates to create and increase wretchedness in any of the parts of society, it is on a wrong system, and reformation is necessary.

Customary language has classed the condition of man under the two descriptions of civilized and uncivilized life. To the one it has ascribed felicity and affluence; to the other, hardship and want. But however our imagination may be impressed by painting and comparison, it is nevertheless true that a great portion of mankind, in what are called civilized countries, are in a state of poverty and wretchedness far below the condition of an

Indian. I speak not of one country, but of all. It is so in England, it is so all over Europe. Let us inquire into the cause. It lies not in any natural defect in the principles of civilization, but in preventing those principles having a universal operation; the consequence of which is a perpetual system of war and expense that drains the country and defeats the general felicity of which civilization is capable.

All the European governments (France now excepted) are constructed, not on the principle of universal civilization, but on the reverse of it. So far as those governments relate to each other, they are in the same condition as we conceive of savage uncivilized life; they put themselves beyond the law as well of God as of man, and are, with respect to principle and reciprocal conduct, like so many individuals in a state of nature.

The inhabitants of every country, under the civilization of laws, easily associate together; but governments being in an uncivilized state and almost continually at war, they pervert the abundance which civilized life produces, to carry on the uncivilized part to a greater extent. By thus ingrafting the barbarism of government upon the internal civilization of a country, it draws from the latter, and more especially from the poor, a great portion of those earnings which should be applied to their own subsistence and comfort. Apart from all reflections of morality and philosophy, it is a melancholy fact that more than one fourth of the labor of mankind is annually consumed by this barbarous system.

What has served to continue this evil is the pecuniary advantage which all the governments of Europe have found in keeping up this state of uncivilization. It affords to them pretenses for power and revenue, for which there would be neither occasion nor apology, if the circle of civilization were rendered complete. Civil government alone, or the government of laws, is not productive of pretenses for many taxes; it operates at home, directly under the eye of the country, and precludes the possibility of much imposition. But when the scene is laid in the uncivilized contention of governments, the field of pretenses is enlarged, and the country, being no longer a judge, is open to every imposition which governments please to act.

Not a thirtieth, scarcely a fortieth part of the taxes which are raised in England are either occasioned by, or applied to, the purposes of civil government. It is not difficult to see that the whole which the actual government does in this respect is to enact laws, and that the country administers and executes them, at its own expense, by means of magistrates, juries, sessions, and assize, over and above the taxes which it pays.

In this view of the case, we have two distinct characters of government; the one, the civil government, or the government of laws, which operates at home; the other, the court or cabinet government, which operates abroad on the rude plan of uncivilized life; the one attended with little charge, the other with boundless extravagance; and so distinct are the two that if the latter were to sink, as it were by a sudden opening of the earth, and totally disappear, the former would not be deranged. It would still proceed because it is the common interest of the nation that it should, and all the means are in practice.

Revolutions, then, have for their object a change in the moral condition of governments, and with this change the burden of public taxes will lessen, and civilization will be left to the enjoyment of that abundance of which it is now deprived.

In contemplating the whole of this subject, I extend my views into the department of commerce. In all my publications, where the matter would admit, I have been an advocate for commerce, because I am a friend to its effects. It is a pacific system, operating to unite mankind by rendering nations, as well as individuals, useful to each other. As to mere theoretical reformation, I have never preached it up. The most effectual process is that of improving the condition of man by means of his interest; and it is on this ground that I take my stand.

If commerce were permitted to act to the universal extent it is capable of, it would extirpate the system of war, and produce a revolution in the uncivilized state of governments. The invention of commerce has arisen since those governments began, and is the greatest approach towards universal civilization that has yet been made by any means not immediately flowing from moral principles.

Whatever has a tendency to promote the civil intercourse of nations, by an exchange of benefits, is a subject as worthy of philosophy as of politics. Commerce is no other than the traffic of two persons, multiplied on a scale of numbers; and by the same rule that nature intended the intercourse of two, she intended that of all. For this purpose she has distributed the materials of manufactures and commerce in various and distant parts of a nation and of the world; and as they cannot be procured by war so cheaply or so commodiously as by commerce, she has rendered the latter the means of extirpating the former.

As the two are nearly the opposites of each other, consequently, the uncivilized state of European governments is injurious to commerce. Every kind of destruction or embarrassment serves to lessen the quantity, and it matters but little in what part of the commercial world the reduction begins. Like blood, it cannot be taken from any of the parts, without being taken from the whole mass in circulation, and all partake of the loss. When the ability in any nation to buy is destroyed, it equally involves the seller. Could the government of England destroy the commerce of all other nations, she would most effectually ruin her own.

It is possible that a nation may be the carrier for the world, but she cannot be the merchant. She cannot be the seller and the buyer of her own merchandise. The ability to buy must reside out of herself; and, therefore, the prosperity of any commercial nation is regulated by the prosperity of the rest. If they are poor, she cannot be rich; and her condition, be it what it may, is an index of the height of the commercial tide in other nations.

That the principles of commerce and its universal operation may be understood, without understanding the practice, is a position that reason will not deny; and it is on this ground only that I argue the subject. It is one thing in the countinghouse, in the world it is another. With respect to its operation, it must necessarily be contemplated as a reciprocal thing, that only one half its powers resides within the nation, and that the whole is as effectually destroyed by destroying the half that resides without, as if the destruction had been committed on that which is within, for neither can act without the other.

When in the last, as well as in former wars, the commerce of England sunk, it was because the general quantity was lessened everywhere; and it now rises because commerce is in a rising state in every nation. If England at this day imports and exports more than at any other period, the nation with which she trades must necessarily do the same; her imports are their exports, and *vice versa.*

There can be no such thing as a nation flourishing alone in commerce; she can only participate; and the destruction of it in any part must necessarily affect all. When, therefore, governments are at war, the attack is made upon the common stock of commerce, and the consequence is the same as if each had attacked his own.

The present increase of commerce is not to be attributed to ministers, or to any political contrivances, but to its own natural operations in consequence of peace. The regular markets had been destroyed, the channels of trade broken up, and the high road of the seas infested with robbers of every nation, and the attention of the world called to other objects. Those interruptions have ceased, and peace has restored the deranged condition of things to their proper order.[1]

It is worth remarking that every nation reckons the balance of trade in its own favor; and therefore something must be irregular in the common ideas upon this subject.

[1] In America the increase of commerce is greater in proportion than in England. It is, at this time, at least one half more than at any period prior to the revolution. The greatest number of vessels cleared out of the port of Philadelphia before the commencement of the war was between eight and nine hundred. In the year 1788 the number was upwards of twelve hundred. As the state of Pennsylvania is estimated as an eighth part of the United States in population, the whole number of vessels must now be nearly ten thousand.

The fact, however, is true according to what is called a balance; and it is from this cause that commerce is universally supported. Every nation feels the advantage, or it would abandon the practice; but the deception lies in the mode of making up the accounts, and in attributing what are called profits to a wrong cause.

Mr. Pitt has sometimes amused himself, by showing what he called a balance of trade from the customhouse books. This mode of calculation not only affords no rule that is true, but one that is false.

In the first place, every cargo that departs from the customhouse appears on the books as an export; and according to the customhouse balance the losses at sea and by foreign failures are all reckoned on the side of the profit, because they appear as exports.

Second, Because the importation by the smuggling trade does not appear on the customhouse books, to arrange against the exports.

No balance, therefore, as applying to superior advantages, can be drawn from these documents; and if we examine the natural operation of commerce, the idea is fallacious; and if true, would soon be injurious. The great support of commerce consists in the balance being a level of benefits among all nations.

Two merchants of different nations trading together will both become rich, and each makes the balance in his own favor; consequently, they do not get rich out of each other; and it is the same with respect to the nations in which they reside. The case must be that each nation must get rich out of its own means, and increase that riches by something which it procures from another in exchange.

If a merchant in England sends an article of English manufacture abroad which costs him a shilling at home, and imports something which sells for two, he makes a balance of one shilling in his own favor; but this is not gained out of the foreign nation or the foreign merchant, for he also does the same by the article he receives, and neither has a balance of advan-

tage upon the other. The original value of the two articles in
their proper countries were but two shillings; but by changing
their places they acquire a new idea of value equal to double
what they had at first, and that increased value is equally
divided.

There is no otherwise a balance on foreign than on domestic
commerce. The merchants of London and Newcastle trade
on the same principle as if they resided in different nations,
and make their balances in the same manner: yet London does
not get rich out of Newcastle any more than Newcastle out of
London: but coals, the merchandise of Newcastle, have an
additional value at London, and London merchandise has the
same at Newcastle.

Though the principle of all commerce is the same, the domestic, in a national view, is the part the most beneficial;
because the whole of the advantages on both sides rest within
the nation; whereas in foreign commerce, it is only a participation of one half.

The most unprofitable of all commerce is that connected
with foreign dominion. To a few individuals it may be beneficial, merely because it is commerce; but to the nation it is a
loss. The expense of maintaining dominion more than absorbs the profits of any trade. It does not increase the general
quantity in the world, but operates to lessen it; and as a greater
mass would be afloat by relinquishing dominion, the participation without the expense would be more valuable than a
greater quantity with it.

But it is impossible to engross commerce by dominion; and
therefore it is still more fallacious. It cannot exist in confined
channels, and necessarily breaks out by regular or irregular
means that defeat the attempt, and to succeed would be still
worse. France, since the revolution, has been more than indifferent as to foreign possessions; and other nations will become the same when they investigate the subject with respect
to commerce.

To the expense of dominion is to be added that of navies,
and when the amount of the two is subtracted from the profits

of commerce it will appear that what is called the balance of trade, even admitting it to exist, is not enjoyed by the nation, but absorbed by the government.

The idea of having navies for the protection of commerce is delusive. It is putting the means of destruction for the means of protection. Commerce needs no other protection than the reciprocal interest which every nation feels in supporting it— it is common stock—it exists by a balance of advantages to all; and the only interruption it meets is from the present uncivilized state of governments, and which is its common interest to reform.[1]

Quitting this subject, I now proceed to other matters. As it is necessary to include England in the prospect of a general reformation, it is proper to inquire into the defects of its government. It is only by each nation reforming its own that the whole can be improved and the full benefit of reformation enjoyed. Only partial advantages can flow from partial reforms.

France and England are the only two countries in Europe where a reformation in government could have successfully begun. The one secure by the ocean, and the other by the immensity of its internal strength, could defy the malignancy of foreign despotism. But it is with revolutions as with commerce, the advantages increase by their becoming general, and double to either what each would receive alone.

As a new system is now opening to the view of the world, the European courts are plotting to counteract it. Alliances, contrary to all former systems, are agitating, and a common interest of courts is forming against the common interest of man. The combination draws a line that runs throughout Europe and presents a cause so entirely new as to exclude all calculations from former circumstances. While despotism

[1] When I saw Mr. Pitt's mode of estimating the balance of trade in one of his parliamentary speeches, he appeared to me to know nothing of the nature and interest of commerce; and no man has more wantonly tortured it than himself. During a period of peace, it has been shackled with the calamities of war. Three times has it been thrown into stagnation, and the vessels unmanned by impressing, within less than four years of peace.

warred with despotism, man had no interest in the contest; but in a cause that unites the soldier with the citizen, and nation with nation, the despotism of courts, though it feels the danger and meditates revenge, is afraid to strike.

No question has arisen within the records of history that pressed with the importance of the present. It is not whether this or that party shall be in or out, or whig or tory, or high or low, shall prevail; but whether man shall inherit his rights, and universal civilization take place—whether the fruits of his labor shall be enjoyed by himself, or consumed by the profligacy of governments—whether robbery shall be banished from courts, and wretchedness from countries.

It is time that nations should be rational and not be governed like animals for the pleasure of their riders. To read the history of kings a man would be almost inclined to suppose that government consisted in stag-hunting, and that every nation paid a million a year to the huntsman. Man ought to have pride or shame enough to blush at being thus imposed upon, and when he feels his proper character, he will. Upon all subjects of this nature there is often passing in the mind a train of ideas he has not yet accustomed himself to encourage and communicate. Restrained by something that puts on the character of prudence, he acts the hypocrite to himself as well as to others. It is, however, curious to observe how soon this spell can be dissolved. A single expression, boldly conceived and uttered, will sometimes put a whole company into their proper feelings, and a whole nation are acted upon in the same manner.

As to the offices of which any civil government may be composed, it matters but little by what names they are described. In the routine of business, as before observed, whether a man be styled a president, a king, an emperor, a senator, or anything else, it is impossible that any service he can perform can merit from a nation more than ten thousand pounds a year; and as no man should be paid beyond his services, so every man of a proper heart will not accept more. Public money ought to be touched with the most scrupulous consciousness of honor. It is not the produce of riches only, but of the hard earnings of labor and poverty. It is drawn even from the bitterness of want and misery. Not a beggar passes, or perishes in the streets, whose mite is not in that mass.

Were it possible that the congress of America could be so lost to their duty and to the interest of their constituents as to offer general Washington, as president of America, a million a year, he would not and he could not accept it. His sense of honor is of another kind.

When it shall be said in any country in the world, my poor are happy: neither ignorance nor distress is to be found among them; my jails are empty of prisoners, my streets of beggars; the aged are not in want, the taxes are not oppressive; the rational world is my friend, because I am the friend of its happiness: when these things can be said, then may that country boast of its constitution and its government.

Within the space of a few years we have seen two revolutions, those of America and France. In the former the contest was long and the conflict severe; in the latter the nation acted with such a consolidated impulse that, having no foreign enemy to contend with, the revolution was complete in power the moment it appeared. From both those instances it is evident that the greatest forces that can be brought into the field of revolutions are reason and common interest. Where these can have the opportunity of acting, opposition dies with fear or crumbles away by conviction. It is a great standing which they have now universally obtained; and we may hereafter hope to see revolutions, or changes in governments, produced with the same quiet operation by which any measure, determinable by reason and discussion is accomplished.

Formerly when divisions arose respecting governments, recourse was had to the sword and a civil war ensued. That savage custom is exploded by the new system, and reference is had to national conventions. Discussion and the general will arbitrates the question, and to this private opinion yields with a good grace, and order is preserved uninterrupted.

Some gentlemen have affected to call the principles, upon which this work and the former part of *The Rights of Man* are founded, "a new-fangled doctrine." The question is not whether these principles are new or old, but whether they are right or wrong. Suppose the former, I will show their effect by a figure easily understood.

It is now towards the middle of February. Were I to take a turn into the country, the trees would present a leafless, wintery appearance. As people are apt to pluck twigs as they go along, I perhaps might do the same, and by chance might observe that a *single bud* on that twig had begun to swell. I should reason very unnaturally, or rather not reason at all, to suppose *this* was the *only* bud in England which had this appearance. Instead of deciding thus, I should instantly conclude that the same appearance was beginning or about to begin everywhere; and though the vegetable sleep will continue longer on some trees and plants than on others, and though some of them may not *blossom* for two or three years, all will be in leaf in the summer, except those which are *rotten*. What pace the political summer may keep with the natural, no human foresight can determine. It is, however, not difficult to perceive that the spring is begun.

GREAT BOOKS IN PHILOSOPHY

PAPERBACK SERIES

John Stuart Mill — *On Liberty*	3.95
John Stuart Mill — *The Subjection of Women*	3.95
John Stuart Mill — *Utilitarianism*	3.95
John Locke — *Second Treatise on Civil Government*	3.95
Niccolo Machiavelli — *The Prince*	3.95
Plato — *The Republic*	5.95
Aristotle — *The Politics*	4.95
Aristotle — *The Nicomachean Ethics*	5.95
Thomas Paine — *Rights of Man*	4.95
Immanuel Kant — *The Fundamental Principles of the Metaphysic of Morals*	3.95

ORDER FORM

The books listed above can be obtained from your book dealer or directly from Prometheus Books. Please check off the appropriate books. Remittance must accompany all orders from individuals. Please include $2.00 postage and handling for the first book and .75 for each additional title. (NYS residents please add applicable sales tax.)

Send to _____
(Please type or print clearly)

Address _____

City _____ State _____ Zip _____

Amount enclosed _____

Prometheus Books

700 E. Amherst St., Buffalo, New York 14215